EVERYTHING UNDER THE SUN

Everything Under the Sun

TOWARD A BRIGHTER FUTURE ON A **SMALL BLUE** PLANET

DAVID SUZUKI

IAN HANINGTON

David Suzuki Foundation

GREYSTONE BOOKS
D&M PUBLISHERS INC.
Vancouver/Toronto/Berkeley

Greystone Books
An imprint of D&M Publishers Inc.
2323 Quebec Street, Suite 201
Vancouver BC Canada V5T 4S7
www.greystonebooks.com

David Suzuki Foundation
219-2211 West 4th Avenue
Vancouver BC Canada V6K 4S2

Cataloguing data available from Library and Archives Canada

ISBN 978-1-55365-528-2 (pbk.)
ISBN 978-1-55365-996-9 (ebook)

Editing by Nancy Flight
Copyediting by Shirarose Wilensky
Cover and text design by Jessica Sullivan
Printed and bound in Canada by Friesens
Distributed in the U.S. by Publishers Group West

We gratefully acknowledge the financial support of the Canada
Council for the Arts, the British Columbia Arts Council, the
Province of British Columbia through the Book Publishing Tax
Credit, and the Government of Canada through the Canada
Book Fund for our publishing activities.

Greystone Books is committed to reducing the consumption
of old-growth forests in the books it publishes. This book is
one step towards that goal.

CONTENTS

Preface

ONE HUNDRED YEARS is not a long time. But if we look at the past century, we see unimaginable change. The human population has grown exponentially, from about one and a half billion to seven billion. People have shifted from rural to urban, and now more than half of us live in cities— up to 80 per cent in developed countries. Automobiles and other amazing technological advances have allowed us to do that and so much more. But we're so involved with our technology that we've designed many of our cities for cars instead of people. Our knowledge and inventions have kept pace with population growth, but that only means they've sometimes sped ahead of our ability to plan more rationally for their use and application. And so we're consuming more, wasting more, polluting more, and using up more of the earth's resources.

Many people are understandably afraid of what we've gotten ourselves into. But we'll never get out of a jam by plugging our fingers in our ears and going "lalalala" or pretending everything's fine. The great scientist Albert Einstein once said, "We cannot solve our problems with the same thinking we used when we created them." Humans are creative and adaptable. We must imagine a brighter future if we are to create it. And we can. But we must apply new ways of thinking and seeing.

Some people view the problems we have created as insurmountable. They believe that our current systems and infrastructure are so entrenched that it would be impossible to do anything but carry on with business as usual. But that would be folly. For the most part, modern living spaces and economies have been built around fossil fuels—for transportation, for distribution of goods and services, for energy to provide us with comforts and products. Even if we didn't have to contend with the problems that our overuse of fossil fuels has created—from pollution to climate change to water contamination to ecosystem disruption to geopolitical instability and social inequity—we still have to remember that supplies of fossil fuels are limited. Even before they run out, they will be found increasingly in places that are more difficult and expensive to reach—as is already happening with deep-sea drilling and tar sands.

Our financial systems have been developed over a short time to contend with the pace of our expanding populations and needs. But they've also become instruments with which to exploit those needs and even to create "needs" that are illusory. The global market isn't just about producing and supplying goods and services to people; it's about reaping profits that create massive disparities in wealth. And that's brought us to an absurd situation where people work more hours to produce goods they don't really need and to earn money to buy more of those goods. It's led to a system based on constant growth and ever-expanding exploitation of finite resources on a finite planet.

It just doesn't make sense anymore.

We often forget how new this economic system is, and how quickly economic systems that aren't working can change. We have progressed from a time when people worked twelve or more hours a day, six days a week, with no vacations or benefits, but we're still harbouring some outmoded thinking from those days. We need to learn from history. It wasn't all that long ago that many of society's leaders in "civilized" countries like the United States believed slavery was essential to the economy. But many people recognized that human rights and dignity are more important than an artificial economic system, and they successfully fought to abolish slavery. And, surprise, it didn't destroy the economy!

Like many previous struggles, protecting our Earth is inextricably linked with issues of social justice. Inequality, poverty, and war are often at the root of environmental problems, and they exacerbate those problems. Exploitation of people and resources around the world has allowed people in developed nations to enjoy a standard of living that is not sustainable. We simply consume too much. And people who have scarcely enough to survive are less likely to worry about large-scale environmental problems. Someone who has to feed a hungry family isn't going to worry about whether an edible plant or animal is endangered.

The global market economy that encourages inequality and exploitation is a recent invention. Note that I said "invention." It is not something real and immutable, like the laws of gravity or thermodynamics. If the economy or any other system that we've invented is not working, then we must change it or replace it. It may sound difficult, but we've done it over and over again throughout our history. That doesn't mean it's easy. Change in the past has often come in the wake of catastrophic wars or revolutions or arms races or space races. But, in the end, it has always involved people sitting down and talking about the problems and the best ways to overcome them. Our hope is to start thinking and talking before catastrophe strikes. Surely we've evolved to the point where we can do that.

With pollution and climate change, species extinction, and destruction of ocean and land ecosystems, we are nearing catastrophe. Some people will deny this, some will say there's nothing we can do about it, and still others will say it's all part of God's plan. But it's happening, and we can and must do something about it. No matter what religious or spiritual beliefs you hold, it's impossible to deny that we have been blessed with a beautiful planet that has everything we need to survive and be healthy. It is up to all of us to care for it and to keep it livable for ourselves and all the living things that share it with us.

Solutions exist. We have the science and technology. We have many intelligent and dedicated people trying to steer us on course. But we need the will and the imagination to change, and, as Einstein said, we need to think in new ways. The problem is more social than technological. We need to commit to adopting ways to live in balance with the natural systems that keep us alive, and with each other. We must recognize that our lives are possible because of a miraculous confluence of time and space, with our planet just far enough away from the sun to provide conditions for us to survive. That sun gives us all of the energy—in one form or another—that we need. Learning how to live well under the sun means finding better ways to use that energy.

This book doesn't have all the answers. But perhaps it can contribute to the conversation, to help people think about the problems we have created and how we might resolve them. This book attempts to identify some of the solutions. But we need more ideas—your ideas. We need to be creative. We need to use our imaginations. We need to talk to each other. This book is an invitation to join the most important conversation of our time.

1

All Creatures
Great and Small

SOME PARENTS HAVE taken me to task for pointing out to their children that we are all animals. It's a basic scientific fact, though. Although we're blessed with large brains relative to our size, we still have a lot in common with other animals. We all need clean air, water, and food to survive. We all have an instinct for survival. But rapid exponential growth in human populations, coupled with economic systems that encourage waste and consumption, means that we often ignore the needs of the other living beings that share this world with us—and we also ignore the fact that we depend on them more than they depend on us. As this chapter shows, in failing to take into consideration our fellow creatures, we also lose sight of what we truly need as humans to survive and to be fulfilled and happy.

· · ·

When mammals are threatened, we are threatened

WE HUMANS SOMETIMES forget that we are animals. We're mammals and, like all mammals, and indeed all animals, we are connected to and dependent on the web of life. When part of that web is in danger, we are all in danger. And our mammal cousins are in danger. According to the International Union for Conservation of Nature (IUCN), one quarter of the world's 5,487 known mammalian species face extinction in 30 years if we don't act now to protect them. This includes many of the planet's apes and monkeys; bears such as polar bears, sun bears, and pandas; and dozens of marine mammals, such as sei and fin whales.

The causes of this biological crisis include habitat loss and damage, introduction of invasive species, pollution, harvesting, and climate change. Because many mammals are large (elephants, hippos, rhinos), exhibit extraordinary intelligence (chimps and gorillas), or have a ferocious nature (lions, tigers, and bears), we have often assumed that they are somewhat resilient to human impacts. This couldn't be further from the truth.

Scientists now believe that the biology of many mammals contributes to their vulnerability. For example, polar bears and grizzlies are particularly susceptible to decline because they require a lot of food for energy, they are large, and they reproduce infrequently and have few offspring when they do reproduce. Human impacts such as unsustainable hunting or habitat destruction put more pressure on the ability of these species to survive.

There is some good news, though. The IUCN assessment showed that "concerted conservation efforts" can bring mammals back from the brink. For example, by reintroducing the black-footed ferret into eight western U.S. states and Mexico, the U.S. Fish and Wildlife Service managed to move the animal from the list of animals that were extinct in the wild to the endangered list.

But who cares about the black-footed ferret, or the wild horse, or the African elephant? We humans are not in danger of extinction, are we? Humans are the most numerous mammal species, and our influence now extends to every square centimetre of this planet, including the atmosphere. But if we think we can survive such a rending of the web of life as the extinction of one quarter of all mammal species, we're living in dreamland. The long-term consequences could be catastrophic because, as the top predator on the planet, our survival and well-being depend on the health and well-being of all life that supports us. (And remember that long-term in this case is only thirty years!)

Even if we look just at the short term, we see that it's in our best interests to protect our fellow animals. As Dr. Jane Smart, head of the IUCN's species program, points out: "The longer we wait, the more expensive it will be to prevent future extinctions. We now know what species are threatened, what the threats are, and where—we have no more excuses to watch from the sidelines." The rapidity and scale of the response to failing financial institutions show that we are capable of action when we perceive danger. Well, the extinction crisis on the planet imperils our very survival.

We must do much more to ensure that all species at risk survive. Besides the mammals, the IUCN added the iconic Pacific sockeye salmon to its red list of endangered species. People on the west coast of North America know that the salmon is the lifeblood of coastal ecosystems, providing food for people, bears, and birds, and fertilizer for the forests. That's a perfect example of how interconnected our web of life is.

We have to make some big changes in the way we do things on this finite planet. We can't just keep destroying habitat, polluting water and air, and killing fish and other animals faster than they can reproduce. And because we are all connected to this fragile web, we need to protect animals and their habitat not just for their sake but for our own as well.

Species loss is a silent epidemic

SCIENTISTS WARN THAT the twin threats of climate change and wildlife extinction threaten our planet's life-support systems, including clean air, clean water, and productive soil. Awareness about the causes and consequences of climate change is growing, leading some governments to look for solutions in areas such as clean energy. Species extinction, however, has gone largely unnoticed by government leaders.

In a June 2010 article in the *Guardian* newspaper titled "Give Decision Makers Access to the Value of Nature's Services," France's ecology secretary and the World Resources Institute's vice-president of science and research argue that "unlike the impacts of climate change, biodiversity—and the ecosystem services it harbours—disappears in a mostly silent, local, and anonymous fashion. This may explain in part why the devastation of nature has triggered fewer alarm bells than a hotting-up planet."

Sadly, this is true. Unlike the devastating forest fires, deadly heat waves, and violent storms that have ravaged the planet as a result of climate change, the disappearance of plants and animals seems to get the attention of politicians only when it results in serious economic and social upheaval—such as when overfishing led to the collapse of cod stocks in Atlantic Canada and orange roughy stocks in New Zealand and Australia, throwing thousands of fishermen out of work.

The unravelling of food webs that have taken millennia to evolve is happening all around us. With every patch of forest cut, wetland drained, or grassland paved over, our actions are destroying wildlife habitat at an unprecedented rate.

Scientists warn that we are in the midst of a human-caused catastrophic wildlife crisis. Of the species we know about, some seventeen thousand plant and animal species are facing extinction, including 12 per cent of birds, 23 per cent of mammals, and 32 per cent of amphibians. Some of the species most vulnerable to human impacts are iconic, well-loved creatures. For example, of the eight distinct bear species that grace our planet, six are now in serious trouble, including sun bears, pandas, and polar bears.

The response of our leaders has, for the most part, been abysmal. The United Nations declared 2010 the International Year of Biodiversity. Countries reported on their progress in reducing biodiversity loss as required under an international treaty called the Convention on Biological Diversity that most nations have signed. However, the UN has admitted that governments have failed to meet the treaty's objectives "to achieve by 2010 a significant reduction of the current rate of biodiversity loss at the global, regional, and national level as a contribution to poverty alleviation and to the benefit of all life on Earth."

Despite our collective failure to meet the 2010 biodiversity target, countries are negotiating new global targets to slow the rate of biodiversity loss. It's easy to be skeptical about the effect these negotiations and meetings in plush hotel ballrooms will have on protecting life on our planet, given the lack of meaningful progress so far. But one outcome of the global biodiversity talks gives us hope.

In 2010, government negotiators from around the world met in Busan, South Korea, where they approved the creation of a new global science body to act as an "early warning system" to inform government leaders on major biodiversity declines and to identify what governments must do to reverse these damaging trends. This global biodiversity scientific body is modelled on the Intergovernmental Panel on Climate Change (IPCC), which, through science, has catalyzed worldwide understanding of and action on global warming.

Despite the efforts of huge multinational oil companies to discredit its work, the IPCC has compiled the best available science on the causes and impacts of global warming and charted the most effective ways for us to solve the problem. In doing so, it has ensured that climate change has remained a priority for governments, and it has proven to be an invaluable tool to help the media understand and report on the issue—independent of politics or PR spin. We hope the newly created "IPCC for nature" will play a similar role in educating, inspiring, and mobilizing policy-makers and the public to take decisive action to stem the biodiversity crisis.

The Year of the Frog

DURING HIGH SCHOOL in Ontario, I spent a lot of time at a swamp near my family's home. Smelling the sweet air in spring, listening to the frogs croak, and catching the insects that would become so important to my life and career gave me solace during those lonely years.

As much as insects became my fascination, I've always loved the frogs. These amazing amphibians occupy a crucial place in the natural order. They are both predator and prey, providing food for larger species and keeping insect populations in balance by eating them. If frogs were to disappear, the planet would soon be covered in flies and other insects. I like flies, but not that much!

In fact, frogs *are* disappearing. Many of us can remember drifting off to sleep to the sound of frogs, but unless we act now, it's unlikely that our children and grandchildren will hear the same lullaby. Scientists estimate that one third to one half of the world's six thousand known amphibian species could go extinct in our lifetime. This would be the largest mass extinction since the disappearance of dinosaurs. More than one hundred species are already believed to have vanished since 1980.

The situation is so critical that conservationists and institutions, including universities, zoos, and aquariums, named 2008 the Year of the Frog. The motto, "Frogs matter. Jump in," is one we should all take to heart. The more we understand about frogs and the reasons for their disappearance, and the more we all get involved in trying to save them, the more likely we will be to head off this impending disaster.

It's not just the frogs we have to worry about. Biologists see frogs and other amphibians as "the canary in the coal mine." Because of their place in the natural order, frogs are often the first species affected by environmental problems and can thus serve as a warning to other species, including our own.

One of the main threats to frogs and amphibians around the world is the spread of a fungus called chytrid (kit-rid), but other factors that we can start to address immediately are also threatening amphibians. These include global warming, habitat loss, pesticide use, pollution, invasive species, and even overuse as food or pets.

Dealing with the fungus will be a challenge. Chytrid is thought to have been spread initially by trading in the African clawed frog, which was used for pregnancy tests from 1934 to the 1950s. The fungus has now infected more than one hundred species of frog, killing them in a way that is still baffling scientists. The spores infect the outer layer of skin, but scientists have yet to figure out its mechanism. Ironically, the fungus is not fatal to the African clawed frog.

In an attempt to ensure the survival of frog species most threatened by the fungus, biologists from zoos, aquariums, and botanical gardens, working with the International Union for Conservation of Nature, set up the Amphibian Ark. Under the program, conservationists have started gathering threatened frogs to breed and protect in captivity. There's no guarantee that the scheme will work, but it's worth a try. One of the challenges will be to maintain genetic diversity under such a program. Another big challenge, though, will come when it's time to put the frogs back. Will there even be places left for them to live? And given the crucial role that frogs play as predators and prey in the natural cycle, what will become of those ecosystems while the frogs are away? Global warming is already shifting the areas where species are found, so when it's time to release the frogs, it might not even be realistic to return them to their former homes.

Those are things we can all work to overcome. Some governments have banned harmful pesticide use for lawns and gardens, which will prevent the deaths of many animals, including frogs. And we can all work to protect the places where animals live, through involvement with conservation groups and by lobbying governments at all levels to ensure habitat is a priority when planning and development decisions are made. Our efforts to slow global warming and to cut down on the waste we produce are also steps that will add up to make a real difference. We must listen to the frogs now, so that our children and grandchildren can listen to them tomorrow.

The macaw, the toucan, and the manduvi

NO MATTER HOW much I learn about nature, I never cease to be amazed by its mystery and complexity. That point really struck me in light of a 2008 study in the journal *Biological Conservation* about the relationship between the hyacinth macaw, the toco toucan, and the manduvi tree, titled "Conservation Puzzle: Endangered Hyacinth Macaw Depends on Its Nest Predator for Reproduction."

The hyacinth macaw is an endangered bird in central Brazil. It has a reputation for being picky when it comes to choosing a home: it lives almost exclusively in natural hollows in manduvi trees, which don't grow in great numbers in the region. In an effort to help preserve the bird and its habitat, Dr. Marco Pizo and his research team at the Universidade do Vale do Rio dos Sinos explored how the manduvi tree's seed is spread. They found that the toco toucan collects and disperses more than 83 per cent of the seeds.

So far, so good. But here's the kicker: the toucan is the macaw's main predator. Besides feeding on the whole seeds of the manduvi, the toucan also has a big appetite for macaw eggs. The researchers also observed toucans taking over macaw hollows and killing the nestlings.

And so, ironically, the macaw depends on its main predator, the toucan, for its survival.

This fascinating relationship has led to what the report's authors call "a conservation biology puzzle," because "any conservation plan for hyacinth macaws must take into account the toucans, which would not normally be done because of their predator status and because toco toucans are not particularly threatened."

It's a puzzle that illustrates the importance of seeing the big picture when it comes to protecting the environment. Attempting to manage a single species in isolation can't work because nature is just too complex. Take the caribou, an iconic species found in Norway, Finland, Siberia, Alaska, and Greenland, and throughout Canada. Caribou are in trouble across their expansive range. In the province of British Columbia, populations of mountain caribou that inhabit the Interior rainforests have plummeted to an estimated nineteen hundred individuals from historic levels of about ten thousand. The main threat is the destruction of its old-growth forest habitat by commercial logging, but scientists believe that predators, like wolves and cougars, may have also played a role in the caribou's decline. Because of this, the B.C. government initiated a plan to kill wolves and other predators, in addition to protecting significant areas of the caribou's habitat. Such "predator control" wildlife management practices are increasingly being proposed or used elsewhere in Canada and in other countries. However, because the science of predator-prey interactions is poorly understood, these methods can have severe and unintended consequences. In the case of the hyacinth macaw, killing its main predator would ensure its demise.

We must understand the broader context if we want our wildlife management plans and conservation efforts to succeed.

Governments have been talking about this "ecosystem approach" for some time, but so far they've been slow to follow the talk with action. The official (and somewhat bureaucratic) name for one area off Canada's west coast acknowledges this approach: the Pacific North Coast Integrated Management Area, or PNCIMA. This 88,000-square-kilometre marine region next to B.C.'s Great Bear Rainforest encompasses the central and north coast and Haida Gwaii and is home to a fascinating variety of life, from basking sharks and blue whales to massive kelp forests and glass-sponge reefs. Although Canada's government has committed to using an ecosystem approach for managing the PNCIMA, it has taken little action to implement the process.

Like the earth's forests, oceans are complex environments where everything is interconnected. Whether on land or at sea, large population changes (including extinction) in one species can have cascading effects throughout the ecosystem.

Good conservation planning requires efforts by local communities and governments at all levels to base decisions on an understanding not just of each species in isolation but of ecosystems as a whole. And we must keep in mind that we're a part of that whole, even though our relationship with nature is often as complex and tricky as the relationship between the hyacinth macaw and the toco toucan.

If the bees disappear, we'll all be stung

SOME PEOPLE THINK of bees as something to be feared.
But without bees, humans would not be able to survive. It's
not just that they provide us with honey and wax; they are
also one of the world's most important pollinators. (In fact,
bees native to North America do not produce honey; most
North American honeybees were imported from Europe—
and not all bees sting!)

Close to 90 per cent of the world's plants rely on pollinators for fertilization and reproduction—including many
of the plants we use for food. Beyond providing food, plants
anchor soil to prevent erosion and fuel the nutrient cycle by
decomposing and absorbing nutrients. Bees aren't the only
pollinators; butterflies, hummingbirds, and bats, among
other animals, provide pollination. But bees are the most
common pollinators. If we lose the bees, we lose the plants,
and if we lose the plants, well...

The problem is we are losing bees. European honeybees,
which are now used for pollination around the world, are
declining in number, as are native North American bees.
We know some, but not all, of the causes. The biggest threat
is habitat loss and destruction, as natural areas are increasingly developed for housing and shopping centres and
sterile lawns. Pesticide use is also killing bees and other
pollinators.

But we can help our buzzing buddies in a number of
ways—and at least one solution is a lot of fun for you and
your kids. First, we can stop using harmful pesticides to
keep our lawns and gardens looking pretty. A growing
number of local governments have been banning these pesticides, known as cosmetic pesticides, not just to protect

pollinators but also to protect human health. As well, a number of large retail stores have voluntarily taken these chemicals off their shelves.

One of the most fun ways we can all work to keep bee populations healthy is to create homes and habitat for the insects. If you have a garden, even a small one on your balcony, you can fill it with plants and flowers that attract bees and other pollinators. And because bees are easy to please, almost any garden will attract them—but remember that native plants will attract native bees and exotic plants will attract honeybees. Choosing a variety of plants that bloom throughout the season will keep bees buzzing from spring through fall.

You can also build homes for bees. Different kinds of bees have different housing needs, and it's a great educational experience to learn how to build homes that will attract various types of bees. Canada and the U.S. are home to hundreds of bee species of all sizes. The smallest is the size of the head of a pin. Some live below ground, some above. And every species is beneficial to plants.

In my hometown of Vancouver, Canada, the Environmental Youth Alliance initiated a project to place mason-bee "condos" throughout the city. Mason bees, also known as blue orchard bees, are small, about the size of a housefly. They are called mason bees because they create rows of cells in their nests divided with walls of clay. They are great pollinators— a single female will visit as many as 17 flowers a minute. In 2008, the EYA handed out 100 bee condos, each housing 36 bees, for residents to place in their yards. The following year, the group put large condos, housing from 72 to 720 bees each, in parks and public spaces around the city. One is even designed to look like an urban condo. By the end of the year, the project had spread more than 8,000 bees across the city.

Urban areas are centres for bee diversity because of the variety of flowering plants, habitats, and landscapes.

As I often point out, everything in nature is interconnected. Bees are a crucial part of this interconnection. If bees start to disappear, the effects will cascade throughout ecosystems, affecting all life, including humans. We must do everything we can to ensure that bees survive and flourish. Our own survival depends on it.

Long live the monarch!

EVERY AUTUMN, TENS of millions of monarch butterflies take wing in southern Ontario, embarking on a miraculous three-thousand-kilometre, two-month journey, arriving in central Mexico in late October and early November. The indigenous people of Mexico believe the returning butterflies carry the souls of ancestors, and November 1 and 2 are celebrated there as the Day of the Dead. Catholic tradition has been syncretized with indigenous observance, so November 1 is All Saints' Day, when the spirits of children return, and November 2 is All Souls' Day, the main Day of the Dead, when the spirits of adults return.

It's a time of celebration, as many Mexicans share a belief with people around the world that a veil is lifted between the living and the dead at this time of year, allowing ancestors to visit for a brief time. We see the origins of Halloween in this belief. It's also a time to celebrate the bounty of the harvest. In fact, the Purépecha indigenous word for the monarch can be translated as "harvest butterfly." The monarch's scientific name, *Danaus plexippus*, means "sleepy transformation," because the butterflies hibernate and metamorphose, from egg to caterpillar to chrysalis to butterfly.

There's also much to celebrate about the monarch butterfly, even though these fragile insects have flown close to the plane of death in recent times. Populations have been reduced by as much as 90 per cent in the past, but there's still hope. That these delicate creatures can make such an arduous journey is in itself a wonderful story of survival and the mysterious workings of nature.

Adult monarchs normally live for just a few weeks. On their northern migration from Mexico, in March and April, they stop along the Gulf Coast of the United States to lay eggs on milkweed, the only source of food for the caterpillars. Over several generations, the butterflies make their way northward, landing on milkweed to lay more eggs along the way. Toward the end of summer, what is known as a "Methuselah" generation is born. These butterflies survive for seven or eight months, and it is they who make the incredible journey south.

Even though they have never been to the volcanic mountains of Mexico, the butterflies are guided by internal compasses and the movement of the sun to the oyamel fir forests where their ancestors spent the winter hibernating before renewing the cycle with their journey northward. During their southward migration, monarchs feed on nectar and help pollinate plants. They let rising columns of air carry them, helping them conserve energy from the nectar. The Methuselah monarchs do not reproduce during migration.

The monarch's relationship with milkweed is interesting. The plant contains a poison that doesn't harm the feeding caterpillars. The monarchs store this poison throughout their lives, which makes them toxic to many, but not all, predators. These predators have learned that the monarch's unique bright orange wings with black veins and white spots signal danger. But this evolutionary artistry isn't enough to protect the monarchs from threats such as logging—legal and illegal—in the forests where they winter, pesticides and herbicides, pollution, storms, parasites and disease, and development and agriculture that eradicate milkweed and nectar-rich flowers.

If we don't protect the forests in Mexico and the milk-weed habitat and nectar sources along its migration routes, the eastern monarch may not survive. Thanks to the efforts of conservation groups, including the World Wildlife Fund and the Mexican Fund for the Conservation of Nature, much of the monarch's winter habitat has been protected as the UNESCO Monarch Butterfly Biosphere Reserve. Even in the reserve, though, illegal logging and storms threaten the monarchs.

We can all help these fascinating creatures—the eastern populations and those that migrate from other parts of Canada to the U.S. and Mexico. To start, we can support conservation efforts and encourage governments to create and protect places where the monarchs feed and breed. Creating pesticide-free monarch way stations or "butterfly gardens" with milkweed and flowers that offer nectar, water, and shelter, in parks, gardens, and schoolyards, is another great way to help the butterflies.

The monarch offers a vivid illustration of the complexity of nature and of the way all of nature is interconnected. And who knows? It may also offer a glimpse of the connection between the worlds of the living and the dead.

Caring for caribou is a matter of urgency

IF YOU'RE IN Canada, you may have a caribou in your pocket. This important icon has appeared on Canada's twenty-five-cent coin since 1937. It would be a tragedy if the coin were the only place you could spot this magnificent animal, though. If we don't protect Canada's boreal forest, that could be the result. The boreal forest extends like a green halo over 35 per cent of the country's northern land mass. Stretching from Newfoundland to the Yukon, it forms the largest uninterrupted, intact forest left on the planet.

This vast region of spruce, aspen, and fir trees, and lakes, river valleys, wetlands, and peat bogs supports three billion migratory songbirds, millions of waterfowl and shorebirds, and is a safe haven for the remaining large predatory animals left on the continent, including wolves, grizzly bears, wolverines, and lynx. Much of this biological richness is at risk from industrial activity such as logging, oil and gas development, mining, and large hydroelectric dams. Among the species most at risk of disappearing is a shy and highly secretive animal called the boreal woodland caribou. It is listed as "threatened" under Canada's Species at Risk Act (SARA).

Caribou are not only well-loved symbols of Canada's identity and a source of national pride; they are also a key indicator of the health of boreal forest ecosystems. When woodland caribou populations start to decline, it's a sure sign that the forests they inhabit are not faring well. Biologists estimate that global caribou populations are less than half of what they were fifty years ago. Canada is no exception. A 2009 federal study by a blue-ribbon panel of caribou biologists found that twenty-nine of the fifty-seven remaining herds of boreal caribou in Canada are not self-sustaining and in some places, like northeastern British Columbia, are on the verge of collapse. The scientific evidence points to two leading factors: expanding industry in the caribou's boreal forest home—including forestry, mining, and oil and gas development—and climate change, which is putting caribou populations under enormous additional strain.

The decline of the boreal caribou is both an ecological and social problem. Not only do caribou play a primary role in the ecology of Canada's boreal forest, they are also important to Aboriginal and Métis people who live in the North. Caribou meat is hearty and rich with calories, and their bones and hides are commonly used for tools and clothing. Many Aboriginal groups also have longstanding spiritual connections with caribou, so the continued persistence of caribou is critical to the ongoing health and well-being of indigenous communities in the North.

Boreal woodland caribou depend on large, intact forest landscapes for their survival. Caribou have already disappeared from half of their historical range in Canada, and scientists believe the probability of many of those herds surviving for the next one hundred years is less than 50 per cent. Herds in Alberta, British Columbia, and the southern Northwest Territories are particularly at risk of extinction because of the intensity of ongoing forestry and energy activity.

For example, one herd in the foothills west of Hinton, Alberta, is now critically endangered. Close to 82 per cent of the Little Smoky herd's habitat is now degraded by a mosaic of clear-cuts; criss-crossed with roads, seismic lines, and oil and gas pipelines; and pockmarked with wellheads. Scientists have determined that this herd, and in fact every herd in Alberta, cannot survive unless we work to protect its current habitat and to restore habitat that has been degraded.

Elsewhere in the boreal, including Ontario and Quebec, levels of industrial activity are quickly approaching similar thresholds of habitat disturbance beyond which caribou can no longer survive without decisive action on the part of federal, provincial, and territorial governments. There is a bright spot: scientists believe that in some large areas, such as the northern Northwest Territories, habitat has not yet been degraded to the point where caribou populations are at risk.

We still have time to ensure that caribou herds do not become extinct. But it will require full and immediate implementation of Canada's provincial, territorial, and federal endangered species laws and accompanying policies. In particular, governments must immediately halt further industrial activities in the ranges of critically endangered herds and must use the findings of the scientists to develop and enact recovery and action plans that identify and protect the habitat that caribou need for food, breeding, migration, and other necessities of survival.

As well as using scientific knowledge, governments must also reach out to Aboriginal people in the boreal who have interacted with the species for millennia. Aboriginal people in Canada have important knowledge about woodland caribou, and governments need to respectfully gather that knowledge and incorporate it into recovery measures for the species. Aboriginal people need to be fully involved in recovery efforts, as the survival of caribou is critical to not only the ecological health of the forest but also the health, culture, and well-being of Aboriginal people who share its boreal habitat.

At a summit meeting in Winnipeg in 2009, Dene Nation president and former Northwest Territories premier Stephen Kakfwi argued that Aboriginal people have a critical role in shaping and leading caribou conservation. "First Nations people have a wealth of intricate land-management knowledge as it applies to caribou," he told delegates from Russia,

Greenland, Norway, and other countries. "Losing caribou is not an intellectual exercise for us and it is not an option. If the caribou are destroyed, our people are destroyed."

Kakfwi also issued a challenge to stakeholders, including non-governmental organizations, industry, and governments, to sit down and work together. "We can't keep fighting each other," he said.

There was a time not long ago when billions of passenger pigeons darkened the skies for days, when huge herds of bison ranged along the centre of the continent, supporting wolves and grizzly bears. Today, caribou are the remnants of the once breathtaking abundance of animals in North America. Are we willing to protect them from becoming mere memories stamped on our coins?

We must fight the alien invasion

IN 2008, CUSTOMS officers at the Vancouver airport got a surprise when they checked the luggage of a woman returning from China. They found seventy live Shanghai hairy crabs! Meanwhile, people in England seem reluctant to flush unwanted goldfish down the toilet, so they give them a new home in the River Thames. Back in my hometown of Vancouver, if you walk through Stanley Park in the summer, you'll come across a pretty spot called Beaver Lake. It's covered in water lilies and is home to red-eared slider turtles and bullfrogs.

What's the common thread? It's all about invasive alien species. These are plants and animals that end up in an environment where they weren't previously found—usually with help from humans—typically causing harm to the native species and ecosystems they interact with. Most invasive species share ecological characteristics that give them an edge over native flora and fauna in competing for resources such as nutrients, light, physical space, water, and food. These characteristics include the ability to reproduce quickly and disperse throughout the environment, as well as tolerance to a range of habitat conditions.

Thus, although the hairy crabs may have been destined for the cooking pot, as the woman claimed, customs officers couldn't take that chance. Environment Canada notes that the crab is one of the one hundred most invasive species in the world. They compete with native species for food; they tunnel into riverbanks and dikes, causing erosion; and they carry parasites that can make people sick.

The Thames goldfish also compete with native species for food and transmit diseases to competing species. In Beaver Lake, the lilies are speeding up the demise of the lake itself, rotting and decaying in the fall and turning the lake into a bog. The UN Convention on Biological Diversity notes that these alien plants and animals constitute "one of the greatest threats to biodiversity, and to the ecological and economic well-being of society and the planet."

Introduction of a species from one environment to another is nothing new. Early European explorers and settlers brought with them to North America livestock and grains that weren't previously found here, as well as stowaway Norway rats and numerous diseases. But globalization and human movement have increased the spread of invasive species worldwide. As with plants and animals introduced by European settlers and explorers, today's invasive plants and animals are sometimes deliberately introduced—often for food or decorative purposes—and are sometimes accidentally introduced, as with zebra mussels and invasive plants spread when ships empty their ballast in Canadian or U.S. waters.

As well as competing for resources, many alien species kill and feed on native plants and animals. They can also alter habitats, making them uninhabitable to plants and animals that previously lived there. And they can breed with native species and weaken the gene pool. The economic impacts can also be severe, as when, for example, valuable food crops or species are wiped out. Because they enter in so many ways, these invaders can't be stopped through laws alone—though laws can help when it comes to things such as regulations governing where and when ships' ballast water can be dumped. Education is one of the best ways to slow the spread. Often, people are unaware of the consequences of introducing new species to an ecosystem.

Cooperation at local and international levels is also essential. Once an introduced species has established itself, it is extremely difficult to eradicate. Targeted control is commonly used where species have already been introduced. This can range from removing the alien species to using pesticides or herbicides to introducing native predator species.

We should all become aware of alien invasive species and the ways they are spread. Many communities have volunteer programs to get rid of these species. In Vancouver's Stanley Park, people volunteer to pull out the invasive English ivy that has grown throughout the park, choking many of the park's native plants. In Maryland, a volunteer program uses a range of methods to eradicate a variety of invasive plants from Swann Park. We can't entirely stop the spread of these alien invaders, but we can all pitch in to make sure we keep our ecosystems as healthy and natural as possible.

B.C.'s trophy hunt is unbearable

FOR MILLENNIA, Aboriginal people have hunted wildlife for food, traditional purposes, and trade. But coastal First Nations in British Columbia argue that killing a threatened animal simply for the thrill of it is foreign to their culture. We call it sport, as if the animals had entered into a life-and-death game. According to Haida leader Guujaaw, "It's not right that anyone should make a sport of killing."

I agree. Grizzlies are officially designated as a threatened species, and black bear subspecies on the B.C. coast are among the most diverse in North America, ranging from the spirit or kermode bear to the Haida black bear. Yet, the B.C. government has ignored pleas from First Nations and conservation groups and has continued to allow these majestic animals to be killed for sport, even in many parks and protected areas and in the Great Bear Rainforest. The results are devastating. As of 2009, in the thirty years that the government has kept records, close to eleven thousand grizzly bears have been killed in B.C., 88 per cent of them by sport hunters. Many are big-game hunters from the U.S. and Europe who pay thousands of dollars to kill a bear in B.C., since these marvellous bruins no longer exist in their own home countries.

First Nations have shared the land with bears for thousands of years. According to Guujaaw, "Bears are as much a part of the environment as we are." Indeed, the bears that feed, breed, and roam among the archipelago of islands and lush mainland valleys of British Columbia play important roles in the ecosystems they inhabit. For example, bears, like other large predatory animals, help regulate prey populations such as deer and thereby prevent overgrazing in forests. Bears feeding on salmon in streams also distribute the nutrients from the fish carcasses across the forest floor. It is a direct transfer of nutrients from the ocean to the forest, and one of the reasons why coastal forests are so rich in biodiversity and why the trees grow to such monstrous sizes.

The ethical and scientific reasons to end the sport hunt are compelling, but so too are the economic arguments. This is particularly true for Aboriginal communities that see the non-consumptive use of bears, such as bear viewing, as potential sources of employment and income for their struggling communities. In 2003, a study by the Centre for Integral Economics showed that grizzly bear viewing brings in twice the income for coastal communities as the trophy hunt. One bear-watching operation in Knight Inlet grossed more than $3 million in direct revenue in 2007—more than all trophy-hunting revenue combined.

"Each bear killed is one less bear that tourists will pay top dollar to photograph," said Dean Wyatt of the Commercial Bear Viewing Association. "Only a total ban on trophy hunting will ensure that bear populations can support the high-end viewing operations that add valuable income to coastal communities."

Protecting opportunities for Aboriginal businesses to participate in the multi-million-dollar ecotourism industry in B.C. must be a priority for government. Art Sterritt, executive director of the Coastal First Nations Turning Point Initiative, argued that government must manage bears to promote sustainable tourism. "This is not a sustainable industry," Sterritt has said of trophy hunting. "It is jeopardizing the sustainable industries we are trying to create."

Killing bears for sport makes no sense scientifically, but it is also unethical and immoral to hunt these animals so that they become a head on a wall or a rug in front of a fireplace when tourists are willing to pay for the chance to photograph them alive and in the wild. Most British Columbians agree. A 2008 McAllister Opinion Research poll found that 79 per cent of B.C. residents believe that to kill a bear simply for the thrill of it is reprehensible and that the practice should end.

Today, the only place you'll find a grizzly bear south of Wyoming is on California's state flag. It would be more than a shame if all we had left to remember these magnificent animals in B.C. were a few films and First Nations carvings.

Hunting in parks is at odds with conservation

IN NATURE, PREDATORS usually go after the weakest of the prey—the oldest or youngest, the injured or ill. It makes sense; these animals are easier to catch, even if they're not always the meatiest. We humans are different. We're often out to prove something, so with our fancy hunting or fishing gear, we go after the biggest and strongest animals—the trophy bucks with bigger horns, the bears with the best coats, or the biggest salmon or halibut.

In the natural order, the predator-prey relationship can ensure that wildlife populations stay strong, as the weakest animals get culled while the strongest and healthiest survive to pass on their genes. Some hunting and harvesting done by humans has the opposite effect. Research published in the *Proceedings of the National Academy of Sciences* shows that many of our current hunting and fishing practices not only reduce population numbers but also cause dramatic and often negative changes in the behaviour, size, and characteristics of targeted species.

Researchers from Canadian and American universities looked at twenty-nine earlier studies, mostly of fish but also of larger animals such as bighorn sheep and even some plants, and found that rates of evolutionary change were as much as three times higher in species that are hunted and harvested by humans.

We've long known that unsustainable rates of hunting and fishing can devastate wildlife populations and fish stocks. Just think of the Atlantic cod fishery and the looming crisis in the Pacific salmon fishery. Now, as the new study shows, we're not just affecting the numbers, we're also having an impact on the characteristics of the animals themselves, such as body size and the age at which they reproduce. We have become a part of the evolutionary process, and that has huge implications when you consider how ignorant we are about the web of living things.

It's an important issue to consider when we look at hunting and fishing practices and regulations. When rules are overhauled to allow hunters to take even more species of animals, we have to think hard about what effect that may have on biodiversity and on evolution.

Although I don't hunt (but I love fishing), I'm not opposed to sustainable hunting and fishing for subsistence and even commercial purposes. But we should be clear: many hunting regulations, especially those that allow hunting in parks, are not about putting venison on the table. They are often at odds with a key principle of sustainable wildlife management: that we should keep *common species common* to ensure they aren't placed at risk in the first place.

Wildlife species around the world are already under enormous pressure, due mainly to habitat loss and fragmentation. We need to act in a precautionary way now to minimize our actions that affect the ability of species to survive and evolve.

Doing the right thing for whales

THE FEW NORTH Atlantic right whales left in the world visit the waters off the east coast of Canada and the U.S. every summer and fall, after migrating from the coasts off Georgia and Florida, where they breed in winter. They're big animals, weighing up to eighty tonnes and measuring up to eighteen metres. But even though the whales enjoy prolonged multi-partner mating and the males have the biggest *cojones* in the animal kingdom, they're slow breeders and haven't been able to increase their number much above four hundred for some time.

Their name was bestowed on them by early whalers, who considered them the "right" whale to hunt because they are large, swim slowly and often close to shore, and usually float when they are killed. Although people haven't hunted them since 1935, we're still putting them in danger from collisions with ships or entanglement in fishing gear in the busy waters off the U.S. and Canada. These factors have made this giant mammal one of the most endangered whales in North America.

But there has been some good news for the North Atlantic right whale. The whale has been listed as endangered in the U.S. since 1973, and its critical habitat has been identified under a recovery plan that was finalized in 1991. Canada's government has been slower to act. The Canadian government released its final recovery strategy for the whales in June 2009, and it includes identification of the whale's critical habitat. Critical habitat refers to areas necessary for a plant or animal species to survive or recover. Under Canada's Species at Risk Act, once an endangered species' critical habitat has been identified in a recovery strategy, the government must legally protect it if it falls within federal jurisdiction, as oceans do.

In the case of the right whale, the government must ensure the whales have a functioning ecosystem that supports their primary needs and that they are protected from collisions with ships and entanglements in fishing gear.

Fisheries and Oceans Canada's original proposed recovery strategy in January 2009 did not identify the Roseway Basin, an area 48 kilometres south of Nova Scotia, as critical habitat. But the David Suzuki Foundation, with advice from Ecojustice, argued that the Roseway Basin and Grand Manan Basin must be included. The revised recovery strategy reflected this advice by adding the Roseway Basin to the critical habitat identification. It's great that the government has moved to protect the habitat of these magnificent mammals, but more needs to be done if our Species at Risk Act is to be effective. A report card issued in April 2009 by conservation groups, including the David Suzuki Foundation, showed that few of the 449 species listed under the act are receiving adequate protection, especially where there might be competing interests.

The Banff Springs snail, which lives in the already protected Banff National Park, is the only animal species to get an action plan since the act became law in late 2002. Three plant species have recently had action plans finalized. Meanwhile, numerous species like the boreal woodland caribou, northern spotted owl, and polar bear continue to disappear with no protection of their critical habitat under

Canada's act. Habitat loss and degradation are the primary causes of decline for 85 per cent of species at risk in the world. Some, such as the polar bear, are protected in the U.S. We can't expect a plant or animal to survive or recover if it doesn't have a healthy and safe place to live.

Of course, governments often find it difficult to put the needs of plants and animals above competing human interests. Protecting critical habitat often means that industrial activities such as logging and mining must be halted or practices significantly improved in areas critical to species' survival. But we often fail to realize that the consequences—both ecological and economic—of losing species and the functioning ecosystems upon which they depend are more severe than the consequences of altering or halting industrial activity within that habitat.

When a species disappears, it affects entire ecosystems. The species may be important as a food source for other animals, or for maintaining the pH of the forest floor, or it may be a predator that keeps other species populations from expanding too rapidly. Functioning ecosystems are far more complex than we realize. Damaging ecosystems that bring us services such as carbon sequestration and storage, pollination, nutrient cycling, and water and air purification tampers with the composition of the natural systems that support wildlife and humans alike.

Some at-risk species in Canada and the rest of the world don't have a lot of time left. We must view the protection strategy for these whales as an example to follow for protecting other endangered species—for their sake and ours.

· · ·

Leaders rally to keep the tiger's future burning bright

THE YEAR OF the Tiger ended in February 2011. Chinese zodiac aside, it wasn't a good year for the tiger. Even golfer Tiger Woods had a better year than his namesake animal. And, as you may know, his year sucked.

The situation for the tiger worldwide has become so precarious that politicians, scientists, conservationists, and bankers from thirteen countries where tigers live met in Russia in November 2010 to discuss ways to save it from extinction. Government leaders from Bangladesh, Bhutan, Cambodia, China, India, Indonesia, Laos, Malaysia, Myanmar, Nepal, Thailand, Vietnam, and Russia signed the St. Petersburg Declaration, with the aim of doubling the world tiger population by 2022—the next Year of the Tiger. The agreement calls for improved habitat protection and enhancement, and a crackdown on illegal poaching and trade in tiger parts.

Three of the nine subspecies of tiger are already extinct and the remaining six are endangered, two of them critically. A century ago, more than 100,000 tigers roamed the eastern hemisphere from the tropical forests of Malaysia to the subarctic woodlands of Siberia. Now, scientists believe only about 3,200 remain in the wild. Like other large iconic predators, including grizzly bears, tigers are threatened especially by habitat loss and fragmentation. But tigers are encountering additional pressures. Tiger skins and body parts are valued by poachers, in part because of their use in traditional Chinese medicine. Increasing conflict with people as human populations expand is also putting the tiger in danger.

As Vancouver writer John Vaillant notes in his excellent book *The Tiger: A True Story of Vengeance and Survival*, it's not just for the tiger's sake that we should be concerned. Vaillant writes that "the tiger represents an enormous canary in the biological coal mine." When a large predator like the tiger, or the grizzly in Canada, is healthy, it's a sign that the habitat and prey that support it are also healthy.

In a November 2010 article for The Tyee news website, "We Can Save the Tiger," Vaillant wrote that the tiger is "a bellwether for what scientists are calling the Sixth Great Extinction: the massive, human-driven loss of species currently underway across the globe." He adds, "If the tiger is allowed to go extinct in the wild (and 'allow' is the operative word here), it will represent the first time in ten thousand years that such a large predator has disappeared from our collective landscape."

Scientists believe the earth has experienced five mass extinctions in its history, all caused by physical forces. This time humans are the cause. Biologists estimate that we are losing about thirty thousand species a year, or about three every hour, through alteration of the landscape and atmosphere, pollution, overexploitation of plants and animals, and introduction of alien species into ecosystems.

With the tiger, we have seen some small successes that should give us hope for the possibility of turning things around. In 1947, Russia became the first country in the world to protect the tiger, and the country's population of Amur, or Siberian, tigers grew from a low of about 30 to 250 in the mid 1980s. As the Soviet Union started crumbling in the late 1980s, the tiger again became threatened because of the ensuing corruption and illegal deforestation and poaching. In 1992, Russia's government implemented new conservation measures, which led to recovery and stabilization of the tiger population at about 450 today.

World leaders now appear to be taking the tiger's fate seriously. With efforts and funding from a number of governments and conservation groups such as the Wildlife Conservation Society, Global Environment Facility, and the World Wildlife Fund, along with donations from individuals including movie star Leonardo DiCaprio, the tiger may be facing a brighter future.

If it is true, as Vaillant points out, that tigers are the bellwether for the Sixth Great Extinction, then we really have little time to lose. Our planet and its natural systems are resilient, but they have recovered from past extinction events only when the cause of those events dissipated. We absolutely must change the way we treat the natural systems of which we are very much a part, or we, as the cause of this impending extinction and as the top predator on the planet, will suffer the consequences.

Aflockalypse now, extinction forever

ON NEW YEAR'S EVE 2011, five thousand red-winged blackbirds dropped out of the sky in Beebe, Arkansas. Necropsies revealed no evidence of poisoning but did indicate the birds had suffered massive internal trauma. Days later, fishermen observed schools of fish floating belly up on Chesapeake Bay. In England, tens of thousands of dead crabs washed up on local beaches, and reports come in almost daily of penguins, turtles, and even dolphins dying unexpectedly in the wild. Are these events signs of the "aflockalypse," as the media dubbed the spate of die-offs? The answer is yes. And no.

Our inherent love and respect for the natural world compels us to take notice when animals die in large numbers, but observations going back more than a century suggest that these mass-mortality events aren't as unusual as we might think, and they are often the result of natural causes, such as adverse weather, disease outbreaks, or stress associated with long-distance migration.

In analyzing bird counts, journal records, and other observations dating back to the late nineteenth century, European researchers found frequent reports of deaths of birds in the hundreds and thousands. One massive kill occurred in spring 1964, when an estimated 100,000 king eiders, representing nearly a tenth of the species' western Canadian population, perished in the Beaufort Sea. These large, beautiful ducks starved when pools of open water in the sea ice re-froze suddenly, preventing them from getting to the food in the water below. More recently, an estimated 40,000 individual birds from 45 different species were killed on April 8, 1993, when a tornado crossed their migration routes off the coast of Louisiana.

Although the sudden death of wildlife in great numbers is alarming, the unravelling of entire food webs is happening all around us and every day—but in a far less obvious manner. With every patch of forest cut, wetland drained, or grassland paved, our ongoing destruction of wildlife habitat is leading to population declines, and even driving some species to extinction.

Climate change is predicted to sharply increase the risk of species extinction within our children's lifetime. According to the Intergovernmental Panel on Climate Change, 20 to 30 per cent of plant and animal species assessed will likely be at increased risk of extinction if global average temperatures continue to rise with escalating emissions of carbon pollution.

This wildlife crisis has been described as a silent epidemic by scientists, like famed Harvard entomologist E.O. Wilson, because it receives so little attention from governments.

The unsettling mass die-offs reveal the inherent vulnerability of wildlife to sudden and dramatic population declines, often as a result of natural causes. This is all the more reason to ensure we don't exacerbate the challenges faced by wildlife in an increasingly busy world. We need to reduce the environmental stressors that we impose on wildlife, so that animals can better cope with and survive the challenges they face every day. We need to eliminate dangerous pesticides and other toxic materials, protect the habitats of endangered plants and animals like caribou, and get serious about tackling climate change.

It's good that people are concerned about sudden animal die-offs, but if we really care about the future of wildlife, we need to start paying more attention to our own role in the extinction crisis—and urge our elected officials to take concrete steps to protect the biological richness with which our planet is blessed.

2

People on
the Move

WE'VE BECOME CITY dwellers. More than half of us
now live in urban areas—up to 80 per cent in industrialized nations—and close to 75 per cent of the greenhouse
gas emissions that cause climate change are produced in
cities. As human populations have grown and moved from
rural communities to cities, so too has the need to find
ways to transport ourselves and the goods on which we
rely. In the developed world, where corporate profits and
new products are often valued above fulfilling our needs,
that has meant the spawning of a car culture. The demand
for private automobiles is now spreading to the developing world, especially in places like China and India, where
growing economies are compelling people to give up bicy-
cles and other forms of transportation for cars. As automakers grew in the twentieth century, along with the oil
and gas industry that kept the cars going, streetcar infrastructure was torn up and replaced by roads, parking lots,
and shopping malls. Now we are seeing the consequences of
our actions: climate change, pollution, gridlock, car-centric

rather than human-centric urban areas, and more. Our car-centric cities and consumer culture are also spawning other problems, including the tremendous amounts of waste we produce. This chapter explores our urban societies and the potential to make cities more livable.

There's no such thing as garbage

IN MEXICO CITY, politicians banned the ubiquitous plastic bags that citizens use for everything from groceries to soft drinks. But that will go only part way to reducing the twelve thousand tonnes of garbage the city produces every day. As of 2009, only 6 per cent of Mexico City's garbage was recycled, but the government has an ambitious plan to recycle, compost, or burn for energy 85 per cent of it by 2013.

Mexico City's waste-management situation illustrates the importance of the three Rs: reduce, reuse, and recycle. And we should add another R: rethink. Many people are getting better at this, but we can do more. Canadians and Americans recycle just over 20 per cent of their garbage. And each Canadian and American produces more than eight hundred kilograms of non-hazardous solid waste a year. That's a lot of garbage going to the landfill, and it's a lot of resources and energy being wasted. Some European countries, such as Austria and Switzerland, are now recycling more than half their waste, so there's a lot of room for improvement. After all, whatever we throw away represents a waste of resources and money—not to mention time.

Beyond the waste problem itself, landfills produce about 25 per cent of methane emissions in Canada and about 17 per cent in the U.S.—and methane is a greenhouse gas more powerful than carbon dioxide. Some cities are now capturing that methane to burn for energy rather than allowing it to escape into the atmosphere. Reducing the amount of trash we create in the first place is the best way to start tackling our waste-management problems. Not only does it mean we send less waste to the landfill, it also means we use fewer resources and less energy—as it takes energy to produce and transport packaging and disposable items.

Every day, more people, stores, and cities are finding ways to cut down on use of disposable plastic bags, but we still create a lot of unnecessary packaging and products. Planned obsolescence—the absurd practice of producing goods that won't last so that the consumer cycle can continue—is still very much with us. We can all avoid buying products that are overpackaged or that are "disposable"— and encourage producers to be more responsible. When we consumers take the time to let stores, businesses, and governments know that we want less packaging and that we want goods that last, we will make a difference. Our changing attitude about plastic bags is a perfect example.

Reusing offers opportunities to get creative. People have always re-tailored clothes to give them new life. Think of the other ways you can use products that no longer function in their intended role. But reusing is an area where some difficulties arise, especially on a larger scale. Reusing waste by converting it to energy is a growing trend. The most common method is burning garbage and using the heat to produce energy. Although the technology is improving, it still has its problems; burning waste creates emissions, for one. And it can turn waste into a lucrative energy commodity, which diminishes the incentive to reduce or recycle. When you really think about it, there is no such thing as garbage. It's all resources of one kind or another, and burning them destroys them forever. Other methods of waste disposal are also being explored, including breaking down the waste with micro-organisms to produce methane and carbon dioxide for biogas.

Recycling is one of the first things that come to mind when we think of waste reduction. Most urbanites in North America dutifully put their paper, plastic, and bottles and cans in the blue box recycling bins. Again, if we use fewer products that must be thrown away, we'll have less stuff to recycle and send to landfills. But we should all be aware that our efforts to recycle are not in vain. If we work to ensure that our communities, schools, and workplaces have good recycling and composting programs and that producers and retailers take responsibility for their products, and if we all improve our own efforts to recycle, we will reduce our need for landfills.

Individual action is important, but legislated solutions are also effective. In Switzerland, people buy stickers that they have to attach to garbage before it is picked up. The more garbage you put out, the more you have to pay. Switzerland now has the highest rate of recycling in the world. We can all do our part as citizens, but, as can be seen in Mexico City and Switzerland, a push by governments can go a long way to creating the kind of large-scale change needed to get our waste-management problem under control.

Making cities more livable may save the world

MORE THAN HALF of the world's seven billion people live in cities. City dwellers consume about three-quarters of the world's energy and generate most of the greenhouse gases that cause climate change. If we are to resolve some of the serious issues around pollution, climate change, human health, and energy consumption, we must look to cities for solutions. As the world's population continues to grow, a shift back to rural living is unlikely. So, what can we do?

Progress in my home city of Vancouver gives me hope, but even here we have a long way to go. The most important move urbanites can make is to get out of their cars. But governments must encourage this with better community design and investments in public transit and pedestrian and cycling infrastructure.

Cycling is the fastest-growing method of travel in Vancouver, thanks in part to a municipal decision to expand bike routes, especially into downtown. Walking is also becoming more popular, with the number of walking trips up 44 per cent since 1994. And increases in the number of people taking public transit are outpacing those in all other urban Canadian centres, with a 20 per cent rise in ridership over the past decade—though government investment in the system has not kept up with this demand, hampering its potential. Transit use is increasing in many U.S. and European cities as well, partly in response to rising gas prices.

Making cities more sustainable isn't just about shifting from car-centric to human-centric planning. Providing incentives to retrofit older buildings or design newer ones to be more energy efficient, encouraging economic activity that doesn't cause a lot of pollution, and creating more parks and green spaces are essential to making cities more livable and less polluting. But steering society away from cars is essential. In his book *Seven Rules for Sustainable Communities: Design Strategies for the Post Carbon World,* University of British Columbia professor Patrick Condon points out that "thirty per cent of the world's carbon dioxide production comes from the United States and

Canada, where only about six per cent of the world's people live. Of this amount, about a quarter comes directly from transportation—and the bulk of that from single-passenger automobiles."

On top of the environmental problems, cars kill. Even though accident rates are going down, thanks in part to technical innovations and regulations around speeding and seatbelt use, cars are a leading cause of death for Canadians and Americans.

The biggest challenges to transforming cities include the entrenched belief among many North Americans that cars are an absolute necessity and the failure of many people to see the benefits of a balanced transportation system. The backlash against a few bike lanes in Vancouver has been strong, even though the lanes have done little to hinder traffic or business.

Vancouver was able to avoid many of the problems other cities face, especially in the U.S., thanks in part to a decision in the late 1960s (spurred by activists) not to expand freeways into the city and to instead focus on a balanced transportation system where walking, biking, and transit are viable options. Statistics Canada reports that Vancouver is the only major Canadian city where commuting times decreased between 1992 and 2005. Cities that focused on expanding roads have seen more traffic and gridlock. As well, Vancouver's transportation emissions, which were once on the rise, have been arrested. Unfortunately, Metro Vancouver still risks repeating the mistakes of other cities, as provincial pressure to expand freeways is ever present. We really need to be more forward thinking.

Condon sums up the opportunities well: "If we change the way cities are built and retrofitted, we can prevent the blackest of the nightmare scenarios from becoming real and can create the conditions for a livable life for our children and grandchildren. It is not apocalyptic to say we can save their lives."

Ride a bike and save the world

Every time I see an adult on a bicycle, I no longer despair for the future of the human race. —H.G. Wells

SCIENCE HAS HAD a tremendous impact on the planet in an incredibly short time. In just the past few hundred of our 150,000 years on Earth, we have invented everything from steam engines, cars, and airplanes to sophisticated weapons and supercomputers. And the pace at which we keep inventing more complex and fascinating machines is increasing. Some of our inventions have been a great boon, some have been harmful, and some, such as cars, have turned out to be a mixed blessing.

But one invention, the bicycle, is so efficient, beneficial, and simple that it may be the best thing we've ever made. A U.K. man even built a bicycle entirely out of wood, with no plastic or metal parts. Everything, including the wheels, gears, and seat, is wood. Inventor Michael Thompson, who made the SplinterBike on a bet with a friend, says it can travel up to fifty kilometres an hour. What's amazing is that, almost two hundred years after the first two-wheeler was made, people are still able to come up with innovative ideas for this practical transportation device.

The modern version of the bicycle with pedals and cranks was invented by French carriage-maker Ernest Michaux in 1861. It's come a long way since then, but whether it's a high-tech racing bike or a one-gear street cruiser, the bike is still a marvel of ingenuity. In fact, it may well be the most efficient form of transportation yet invented.

The best part of the bike is that you, the rider, are the engine. The fuel is what you eat and drink. Putting the human engine together with the gears, wheels, and frame of a bike gives you a mode of transportation that uses less energy even than walking. As for our most popular method of getting around—the automobile—there's no comparison. According to the Worldwatch Institute, a bicycle needs 35 calories per passenger-mile, whereas a car uses 1,860. Buses and trains are somewhere in between.

It's worth thinking about the potential this amazing invention offers. With oil prices climbing and environmental damage from car emissions increasing, bikes are becoming a more attractive form of urban transportation every day. Cleaner air, reduced congestion, safer streets, and lower noise levels are just a few of the benefits. When people get out of their cars and onto their bikes, they'll also become fitter, leading to lower health-care spending. And as more people take up cycling, it also becomes safer. Although, those who worry about the safety of cycling might be interested in a British Medical Association study that found the health risks of inactivity are twenty times greater than the risks from cycling.

The money that could be saved nationally on things like health care—not to mention the infrastructure required to keep so many cars on the road—reaches into the billions, but the money an individual can save on fuel, insurance, and maintenance costs alone is also substantial. And because biking is a lot of fun, it will probably increase what the people of Bhutan call "gross national happiness"!

But we still have a ways to go. Canadians and Americans use bikes for fewer than one in a hundred trips—though in

Vancouver it's a bit higher, at about 4 per cent. Compare that with the 20 to 35 per cent of trips taken by bike in the European Union and 50 per cent in China. (Unfortunately, the trend is reversing in China as the country embraces car culture.)

Shifting from car dependence will take action at the individual level, with more people simply deciding to get on their bikes, but governments must also do more to make it easier for people to ride bikes. And they can. In just three years, from 1998 to 2001, Mayor Enrique Peñalosa of Bogotá, Colombia, turned his city of 6.5 million from a gridlocked parking lot into a city where public spaces live up to their name. He did this by restricting car use, increasing gas taxes, and building hundreds of kilometres of bike and pedestrian paths, as well as investing in buses.

Making our streets safer for cyclists by giving them space to ride is an essential first step. The investment required is far less than that required for infrastructure for cars. Tax breaks for cyclists also help, and employers can offer secure bike parking and showers for those who work up a sweat on the way to work. For employers, the benefits of encouraging cycling are numerous. A Dutch study found that people who cycle to work take fewer sick days, and research has shown they are generally happier and less stressed. Cyclists can also avoid traffic jams and are not as likely to be late for work. And bike lock-ups cost far less than car parks.

Of course, cycling isn't a panacea. In many parts of the world, the weather isn't always conducive to cycling. And not everyone has the strength to ride up the hills in some cities. But if more of us choose bikes whenever possible, and use public transport or at least energy-efficient vehicles when we can't ride, we'll all be much better off.

Bicycling infrastructure pays dividends

MOST ARGUMENTS AGAINST bike lanes are absurd. Consider this: we have wide roads everywhere to accommodate cars, most of which carry only one person. On either side of many of those roads, we have pedestrian sidewalks. In most large urban areas, we also have bus lanes and transit systems such as subways and rapid transit. When cyclists ride on roads, drivers often get annoyed. If they ride on sidewalks, pedestrians rightly get angry.

Human-powered transportation will get only more popular as gas prices rise and as the negative consequences of our car-centric culture increase. We should be doing everything we can to discourage single-occupant automobile use while encouraging public transit and pedestrian and pedal-powered movement.

In many North American cities, including Vancouver, commuters scream bloody murder if it takes them an extra two minutes to get to their destination by car. The reality is that drivers are slowed more by increases in car traffic than by bike lanes. According to the *Globe and Mail*, a 2009 study by Stantec Consulting Ltd. found that traffic delays because of bike lanes in Vancouver were mostly imagined. Drivers who were surveyed thought it took them five minutes longer to travel along a street with a new bike lane. But the study showed that it actually took from five seconds less to just a minute and thirty-seven seconds more.

There's also the argument that slowing car traffic down is a good thing. In some European cities, planners are finding that making life more difficult for drivers while providing incentives for people to take transit, walk, or cycle creates numerous benefits, from reducing pollution and smog-related health problems to cutting greenhouse gas emissions and making cities safer and friendlier.

In Zurich, Switzerland, planners have added traffic lights, including some that transit operators can change in their favour, increased the time of red lights and decreased the greens, removed pedestrian underpasses, slowed speed limits, reduced parking, and banned cars from many streets. "Our goal is to reconquer public space for pedestrians, not to make it easy for drivers," chief traffic planner Andy Fellmann told the *New York Times*. In June 2011 he also noted that a person in a car takes up 115 cubic metres of urban space in Zurich whereas a pedestrian takes 3.

Where streets were closed to cars in Zurich, store owners worried about losing business, but the opposite happened—pedestrian traffic increased 30 to 40 per cent, bringing more people into stores and businesses. In Vancouver, the Stantec study found that businesses along new downtown bike routes initially experienced minor decreases in sales but that numerous strategies were available to overcome the declines. In the long run, most cities that have improved cycling and pedestrian infrastructure have seen benefits for area businesses.

Building bike lanes also creates jobs and other economic spinoffs, according to a June 2011 study from the Political Economy Research Institute in Amherst, Massachusetts, titled "Pedestrian and Bicycle Infrastructure: A National Study of Employment Impacts." Researchers found that "bicycling infrastructure creates the most jobs for a given level of spending." For every $1 million spent, cycling projects created an average of 11.4 jobs in the state where the project was located, pedestrian-only projects created about 10 jobs, and multi-use trails created about 9.6 jobs. Infrastructure combining road construction with pedestrian and bicycle facilities created slightly fewer jobs for the same amount of spending, and road-only projects created the least, with a total of 7.8 jobs per $1 million. One of the main reasons is that more of the money for road building goes to materials and equipment, whereas with bicycle and pedestrian infrastructure more goes to wages and salaries.

It's important to note that European cities have matched disincentives to drive with improved public transit. After all, not everyone can get to his or her destination by walking or cycling. But with fewer cars and reduced gridlock, those who must use automobiles—including service and emergency-response vehicles and taxis—have an easier time getting around.

Fortunately, the backlash against cycling infrastructure improvements appears to be subsiding. As oil becomes scarce and pollution and climate change increase, people are finally realizing that transporting a ninety-kilogram person in two tonnes of metal just isn't sustainable, especially in urban areas.

If there's a war on cars, which side is winning?

WE HUMANS LIKE our wars. We have a war on drugs, a war on terror, a war on crime, and now, it seems, a war on cars. The last "war" has entered the political vocabulary in Vancouver, where city council has been trying to reduce reliance on private automobiles; in Toronto, where the mayor is driving the agenda in the opposite direction; and in Seattle, where bike lanes and increased parking fees have come under fire. In the U.K., they've been calling it a war on motorists.

It's not really much of a war, though. If anything, it's just a bit of catch-up to create better public spaces and to allow more sensible forms of transportation some room in our car-dominated cities. Let's take a look at some of the battle-fields—and the casualties.

In Vancouver, opponents and local media predicted "chaos" from a bike lane on the Burrard Bridge, which connects the city's downtown with the West Side. After the chaos failed to emerge, opponents, rather than learning from experience, went on to predict the same thing for other bike lanes in the city, mostly in the downtown core. Despite a few bumps, the chaos has yet to reveal itself. At the same time, the provincial government is spending $3 billion on a new ten-lane bridge and expanded highways to move cars and trucks in and out of the city.

In Seattle, in addition to a few new bike lanes and a slight increase in downtown parking rates, politicians are considering spending $7 billion on a new bridge and a new tunnel to keep the cars and trucks moving.

Nowhere has the term been more ubiquitous than in Toronto, where it became a rallying cry leading up to and during the 2010 civic election. Numerous headlines in business-friendly newspapers raised the alarm about the city's war on cars, with one newspaper even referring to it as a "nutty war on cars." It was all because the city council of the day was spending money on public transit and bicycle and pedestrian infrastructure and, according to opponents, not enough "to make it easier for cars to move throughout the city."

If there is or has been a war on cars, the cars are winning. Cars—often with a single occupant—still rule our cities and roadways, and they're still relatively inexpensive to operate. And despite minor reductions in parking in cities like Vancouver to make way for bike and pedestrian infrastructure, most North American cities still devote way more valuable land to parking spaces than necessary. In the U.S., there are eight parking spaces for every car. We also devote an incredible amount of real estate to our ever-expanding road systems, often at the expense of public spaces.

As for casualties, 32 per cent of the 44,192 accidental deaths in Canada between 2000 and 2004 were from motor-vehicle accidents, 70 per cent among people age 15 to 24, according to Statistics Canada. Add to that the numerous injuries caused by vehicle accidents—often caused when cars come into contact with pedestrians and cyclists—and you get a pretty good idea of which side has the upper hand in this "war." And much of the health-damaging pollution and greenhouse gas emissions that contribute to dangerous climate change come from private automobiles.

So, if there were a war on cars, we would have to conclude that people are on the losing end. Of course, there is no war on cars. The only battle regarding cars is a propaganda war and, as *Guardian* writer George Monbiot points out in a January 2011 article, "The Imaginary War," it's "about private interests trumping the public interest, about allowing people to pursue their desires, regardless of the cost to society." Maybe it's time we really did wage a war on cars.

Car culture is unsustainable

ARE WE DRIVING ourselves into oblivion? Or will new automobile technology save us from the environmental impact of the fossil-fuelled tanks we use to get around?

On the extreme end of the consequences of our car-centric societies, we need only to look at the massive traffic jam in China in 2010 that stretched for one hundred kilometres and lasted almost two weeks. Apparently it's becoming a common occurrence in China, where use of the private automobile and truck transport are increasing.

On the brighter side, automobile technology has improved a lot over the past few years, partly in response to stricter fuel-emissions standards in some countries, including Canada and the U.S. But is it enough? We've had commercially available hybrid cars now for more than a decade, but they still use fossil fuels. Electric-car technology is picking up, but it doesn't resolve all of the issues, especially as the electricity still must come from somewhere, and, in many places, that means coal-fired power plants. Car manufacturing is also energy intensive.

To resolve some of these issues, an Alberta company has developed an electric car made out of hemp fibre. Beyond reductions in fossil-fuel use to power the car, the materials used to manufacture it are also more sustainable. Hemp grows easily outdoors with little water or pesticides, and it can be used in lightweight but durable composites to build the cars.

One invention that partly avoids the problem of charging electric car batteries by using electricity sources that may contribute to greenhouse gas emissions is U.S. inventor Charles Greenwood's inexpensive HumanCar. It can operate as an exercise-based, human-powered vehicle or a plug-in hybrid electric. Power can be generated by one to four people who "row" the car. It can reach speeds of up to one hundred kilometres an hour. Of course, it has its drawbacks, especially as one must be pretty healthy to operate it. Cars powered by solar cells and hydrogen are also being developed, along with cars that use alternatives to fossil fuels, such as ethanol or biodiesel.

The need for solutions is obvious. Cars not only contribute to air pollution and greenhouse gas emissions, but they also cause water pollution from fuel-storage leaks, improper disposal of oil, and runoff from roads that washes into rivers, lakes, and oceans. Noise pollution, death from road accidents, and the impact of cars on the shape of urban environments are all issues as well.

Technological developments are welcome, but maybe it's time we started rethinking our car culture as a whole. The average car in North America carries 1.5 people, which means that most cars on the road have only a driver in them. Is it really efficient to use more than two thousand kilograms of metal to transport ninety kilograms of human? A life-cycle analysis, which takes into account manufacture and disposal, as well as operation, shows that cars are inefficient products.

We aren't likely to do away with private cars in the near future, especially in rural areas with low population density. But we can at least start to think differently about our "need" for them. That means improvements to public transit, urban design that is less car-centric, and other innovative ideas to reduce our reliance. Walking and cycling when possible is also great, and it improves health. When we must drive, we should try to use cars that are fuel efficient, and drive in ways that cut down on fuel use, such as combining trips and shutting the car off rather than idling when stopped. Even in China, it's not all bad news. Although car culture is growing, the use of electric bikes is exploding. In 2008, people in China bought 21 million e-bikes, compared with 9.4 million cars. China now has 120 million electric bikes on the road, up from about fifty thousand a decade ago.

We take our cars for granted, but really, they haven't been a part of our human culture for that long, and they needn't be an essential part forever.

3

Healing Energy

ALL ENERGY COMES from the sun. No, we haven't made the switch to 100 per cent solar, but every form of energy relies on the sun. Even fossil fuels represent a form of solar energy. Hundreds of millions of years ago, plants and animals retained energy from the sun when they died. Buried and compressed for millennia, their energy concentrated as hydrocarbons to form coal and oil. We burn these materials to release the energy stored within them. Wind energy is also a function of sunlight. When the sun warms the earth's atmosphere, it creates wind, which can turn turbines to produce electricity. The amount and sources of energy we use all have impacts. Fossil fuels have created the most immediate danger, with threats of climate change and pollution, as well as dwindling supplies. We must conserve energy, and we must explore safer, sustainable alternatives if we are to continue to live well on this planet.

. . .

Japan's crisis offers energy lessons

THE MASSIVE EARTHQUAKE and subsequent tsunami that hit Japan in 2011 were horrendous and heart-wrenching, and our thoughts went out to the people of that country as they coped with the aftermath and the terrible losses they suffered. To make matters worse, the terrifying natural disaster has sparked a human-caused crisis, as radiation leaked from crippled reactors at the Fukushima Daiichi nuclear power plant.

Although our immediate concern was and is for the people of Japan, we must also draw lessons from this misfortune. First, we can learn from the Japanese about being prepared. As horrific as the earthquake and its aftermath were, the situation could have been far worse if the Japanese people took the same complacent approach to disaster planning that many people in other parts of the world, including North America, follow. But it's also another indicator that we have to take a close look at our energy systems.

In 2010, the world watched another energy-related calamity unfold as oil spewed into the Gulf of Mexico after an explosion on the *Deepwater Horizon* drilling platform. Both the nuclear crisis in Japan and the oil spill in the Gulf focused our attention on the things that can go wrong in our insatiable pursuit of cheap energy. But the issues around our energy use are far more serious and persistent. They include pollution, political instability, rising costs, and climate change.

Once again, our energy appetite has provoked a global nightmare. We can sink deeper into crisis, or we can use it as an opportunity to look at ways to achieve a sustainable energy future. Fossil and nuclear fuels are finite and therefore cannot be truly sustainable. They will run out, and we're already seeing one of the outcomes of depleting supplies: skyrocketing prices. Another consequence is that we will have to rely increasingly on oil from difficult sources (environmentally and politically), such as deeper water, the tar sands, the Arctic, and volatile political jurisdictions. Using fossil and nuclear fuels also creates enormous problems now and into the future as greenhouse gases and radioactive and long-lived wastes accumulate.

In addition, fossil and nuclear fuels are not equitably distributed throughout the world. Oil deposits, for example, are often found in geopolitically unstable areas. And nuclear energy has proven to be incredibly expensive and time-consuming to get into production. If the money proposed to refurbish aging facilities and build new ones were put toward renewable energy from wind, solar, and geothermal, the impact would be immediate and would get us moving toward a truly sustainable energy future.

The need to assess our energy options is more important than ever. All have consequences and tradeoffs. Climate change caused by burning fossil fuels endangers our planet, nuclear disasters and nuclear waste are potentially significant threats to our health and ecosystems, and even renewable sources have impacts. It's time we took a close look at our energy use to find better ways of providing for our needs. We can all start doing our part by using less.

A nuclear reaction

ONE COULD BE forgiven for thinking we've overcome the problems associated with nuclear power. Everywhere you turn, nuclear is being touted as a "green" energy source and a solution to global warming. Canada's prime minister, Stephen Harper, sang the benefits of both nuclear power and uranium mining in a speech to a business crowd in London, England, in 2008. "As the largest producer of uranium, we can contribute to the renaissance of nuclear energy, a no-emissions source that will be expanding here in Britain and around the world," he said.

If only it were so easy. The Fukushima nuclear disaster, and earlier disasters like Chernobyl and Three Mile Island, reminds us of issues like nuclear waste, nuclear-weapons proliferation, accidents, and pollution from uranium mining.

Have those problems gone away? Has science found a way to deal with them? Unfortunately, the answer is no—and those aren't the only problems. Nuclear power is also expensive and heavily subsidized by taxpayers' money, and it isn't even totally emissions-free. Although nuclear energy's ability to provide large-scale continuous power makes it tempting, we should consider better ways to deal with our energy needs.

To start, waste from uranium mining and nuclear power plants is a serious issue, especially considering that much of that waste is highly radioactive. Although we can recycle some waste from power production, we still haven't really figured out what to do with most of it. One method for large-scale storage is to bury it, but that's basically a policy of out-of-sight, out-of-mind—we don't yet know the full consequences. It's also expensive and the waste has to be transported over long distances where the probability of a mishap is very real. And although nuclear has a relatively good safety record compared with some other large-scale energy technologies, the consequences of an accident can be far worse—as we learned with Fukushima and in 1986 when a reactor at a nuclear power plant in Chernobyl, Russia, exploded. The Chernobyl disaster sent radioactive fallout into the air over Russia, Europe, and even parts of North

America and led to an increase in cancers in the areas with the highest concentrations of fallout. We're still assessing the damage from Fukushima.

If nuclear energy really does expand around the world, as many people hope, the dangers of weapons proliferation will continue to grow. Nuclear power plants also take a long time to build and are incredibly expensive—and are notorious for going massively over budget. Canada alone has subsidized the nuclear power industry to the tune of $20 billion over the past fifty years. Just think of what we could have done by putting that kind of money into renewable energy.

Nuclear energy isn't even all that green when it comes to global warming. If you look at the life cycle of nuclear power plants, the technology produces greenhouse gases at every step, from energy-intensive uranium mining and transportation to constructing and decommissioning power plants. (Looking at the life cycle of energy technologies hasn't always been a common practice, but it's an important step that has allowed us to identify problems with energy sources that look attractive at first glance, such as corn-based biofuels.)

If we were to look forward instead of backward, Canada and the U.S. could become leaders in energy technology and innovation. As costs for renewable energy go down, costs for old-school technologies like nuclear power and fossil fuels continue to rise. Advances have also been made in power-grid management, meaning renewable sources can be more easily integrated into energy systems.

One should also keep in mind that uranium is a limited resource. The European Commission estimated in 2001 that global supplies of uranium could last as few as twelve years if capacity increases substantially and will last only from about forty to seventy years with current usage rates. Prices have already been skyrocketing as uranium becomes scarce.

As we rethink our energy future in light of the dangers of further increasing greenhouse gases, we have an enormous opportunity. I believe that rather than putting all of our faith in big technology (big dams, coal plants, nuclear power), investing in a decentralized grid of diverse, small-scale renewable energy sources would be far more resilient and reliable.

We should all get behind renewable energy in order to avoid the dangers and expense of an expanding nuclear industry. But there's something else we can do: use less energy. Conservation means we could avoid having to build expensive power plants, and we'd also have cleaner air and some real solutions to global warming. Many people have already switched to more energy-efficient appliances and are finding other ways to reduce energy consumption. All of those small things add up to make a big difference. People really do have the power.

Scheer determination transformed Germany's energy grid

IN 2005, I ATTENDED an international conference in Montreal on the Kyoto Protocol. There, I heard a speech by German parliamentarian Hermann Scheer. I knew nothing about him, but as I listened to him talk about how Germany had become the world's leading exporter of wind technology and was on its way to phasing out its nuclear reactors, I was blown away. Here was a politician who articulated the obvious realities about energy: fossil fuels are finite and will run out, the biggest sources of oil are often in the most politically volatile regions, nuclear energy is also non-renewable and bequeaths a legacy of radioactive waste for thousands of generations, and the sun provides free, clean energy in abundance to all nations.

Sadly, Scheer died in 2010 at the age of sixty-six. Over the years, I got to know this canny, fearless politician who stayed true to his beliefs and became so popular he didn't have to play party politics. The problem of energy, he once told me in Berlin, is not technological; it is political in the broadest sense. Once the decision is made to exploit a particular form of energy—nuclear, hydro, fossil fuels, renewable—all kinds of expertise and infrastructure are built up.

So, for example, once the decision is made to use oil, geologists are needed to find the oil, extraction methods must be developed, the crude has to be refined, delivery systems must get the oil to consumers, gas stations must be built, and so on. All of these levels now have a huge stake in the oil industry, so it's not surprising that when someone suggests that alternative energy sources like sunlight have many advantages over fossil fuels, the response is "ludicrous," "impossible," "it will never contribute more than a fraction of our needs," "unreliable," "too expensive," and on and on. What Scheer meant by political, I believe, is the mindset that results from having such a heavy investment in the status quo.

After the Organization of Petroleum Exporting Countries (OPEC) oil embargo in 1973, Scheer, who had a doctorate in economics, realized that energy was a major weakness in Germany's industrial future. The country didn't have oil reserves or large rivers for hydroelectric projects and so was generating electricity with nuclear and coal plants. He realized that this made Germany vulnerable to the vagaries of geopolitics and that these were not sustainable forms of energy.

He recognized that the sun radiates more than enough energy and that this energy from the sun and secondary sources like wind, waves, and biomass are sustainable. Even though he was a politician, Scheer founded the non-profit EUROSOLAR to encourage renewable-energy initiatives in all sectors of society. His efforts, which coincided with the rise of the anti-nuclear Green Party in Germany, struck a chord. Could renewable energy provide enough energy to shut down all nuclear plants? Scheer knew it could, even though scientists and other "experts" declared it was impossible for renewables to account for more than a small percentage of the nation's electricity.

With the Green Party holding the balance of power in a left-wing coalition government, Scheer was able to introduce an innovative plan: a feed-in tariff, which committed the country to accept all renewable energy (primarily wind and solar) onto the grid and to guarantee a premium price for that energy for twenty years. That provided a huge incentive for individuals or co-ops to build turbines and install solar panels because banks would not hesitate to provide loans given those conditions.

As a 2008 article in the *Globe and Mail* noted, the feed-in tariff, beyond giving Germany more than twenty thousand megawatts of clean energy, also created new economic opportunities. As of 2008, the renewable-energy sector generated "about $240 billion in annual revenues and [employed] a quarter-million Germans. Germany's wind industry created eight thousand jobs in 2007 alone, and one study suggested that the renewable sector could provide more work than the auto industry (currently the nation's biggest employer) by 2020."

Many people have been calling for a switch to renewable energy. Nobel laureate and former U.S. vice-president Al Gore has called on the U.S. to work toward switching to 100 per cent renewable energy before 2020. In response, we've heard the same old tune from a chorus of stuck-in-the-oil naysayers. Too bad they didn't get the chance to meet Hermann Scheer.

Wind power is healthier than the alternative

WIND ENERGY IS increasingly being considered a viable and attractive power source. Many countries, including the U.S., Germany, Spain, China, and India, are putting policies into place to drive the development of their wind energy industries. However, a backlash has been growing in many places where wind power is being developed. One of the criticisms of wind development has been its impact on human health, mostly because of the noise that wind turbines produce. Yet, the peer-reviewed scientific research indicates that the sound from windmills, which generally falls into three categories (audible sound, low frequency, and infrasound), has little to no impact on human health.

This is especially true if windmills are built far enough away from residences. For example, the required setback in Ontario, Canada, is 550 metres. At this distance, the audible sound from windmills has been found to be below 40 decibels, which is around the level of sound you'd find in most bedrooms and living rooms. Studies from the University of Massachusetts similarly found that even if the sound were audible, annoyance would be minimal.

Critics have also pointed to low-frequency sound and infrasound as the source of health impacts from wind turbines. These are sounds that are either difficult to hear or inaudible to humans. However, Ontario's chief medical officer of health did a review of the scientific literature and found no evidence that low frequency sound from wind turbines causes adverse health effects.

Research from Sweden and the Netherlands may shed some light on the opposition that windmills are facing, despite the lack of evidence for human health impacts. At or just under forty decibels, 73 per cent of people could notice the sound and 6 per cent were annoyed. But those who did not like windmills or found them ugly were more likely to notice the sound and were more likely to be annoyed by it. Although we should always remain open-minded about new and emerging research on any issue, the evidence seems clear that wind turbines built with appropriate setbacks do not constitute a health hazard. And wind becomes a more attractive energy source when you consider the health impacts of the main energy alternative, burning coal and other fossil fuels.

According to the World Health Organization, air pollution is responsible for two million premature deaths a year. It also sends a lot of people to emergency rooms and doctors' offices. When considering the complaints that get raised about wind power, we should heed the conclusion of Maine's Center for Disease Control. After dismissing the notion of a moratorium on wind development because of its health impacts, the center's Dr. Dora Anne Mills concluded, "If there is any evidence for a moratorium, it is most likely on further use of fossil fuels, given their known and common effects on the health of our population."

As for the impacts on wildlife, that's another story. But most scientific research shows that newer technologies and proper locating can overcome most of the threats to birds and bats. One study also noted that "the number of birds killed in wind developments is substantially lower relative to estimated annual bird casualty rates from a variety of other anthropogenic factors, including vehicles, buildings and windows, power transmission lines, communication towers, toxic chemicals including pesticides, and feral and domestic cats."

It's never easy to find energy technologies that will satisfy everyone, but with the world facing ever-growing negative consequences of burning fossil fuels, we must weigh our options. In doing so, wind power comes out ahead. If we ensure that care is taken to use technologies with minimal environmental impact and to locate turbines in areas where effects on humans and animals are also minimal, there is no good reason to oppose wind power.

The trouble with tar sands

IF YOU WANT to be scared, you don't need to watch a horror movie or read the latest Stephen King bestseller. Real terror can be found by simply firing up Google Earth, the computer program that allows users to look at satellite pictures of any place on the planet. By mousing over and zooming in, you can see what Alberta's tar sands look like from space.

It is not a pretty sight. In fact, it's scary—and for good reason.

A book by celebrated journalist Andrew Nikiforuk, *Tar Sands: Dirty Oil and the Future of a Continent*, explores what these grey spots on Google Earth mean to Canada's environment and economy. It's an important book, one that every Canadian should read to find out how the world's largest energy project will affect us.

The scale of the Alberta tar sands project is unprecedented in Canadian history. Alberta's "blue-eyed sheiks," as the oil-industry elite are known, stand to make billions of dollars from carving up northern Alberta in order to meet U.S. and global demand for oil. But these dollars pale in comparison with the environmental value that is being squandered at the expense of petro dollars.

The main tar sands deposits are at three sites in Alberta: Peace River, Cold Lake, and Athabasca. The Athabasca region contains the largest deposit of crude bitumen in the world. All of this bitumen, a complex mixture of molecules from prehistoric life, is a geological miracle with which Canada has been blessed. This bitumen could turn out to be a substance that will help our children and grandchildren in ways that we can't even imagine today, much the same way our ancestors couldn't have imagined us using silicon in our computer chips. But instead of safeguarding this resource, we are quickly using it up. And we are creating an environmental catastrophe that will take centuries to recover from ... if we recover at all.

The tar sands consist of a mixture of silica sand, minerals, clay, water, and, most importantly, crude bitumen. The process of converting bitumen so that we can use it to power our cars, heat our homes, and transport our food is not easy. It's estimated that two tonnes of earth must be excavated to produce one barrel of thick, tar-like bitumen. And it requires as much as three barrels of fresh water from the Athabasca River to make one barrel of bitumen. It also takes a huge amount of energy to extract the oil from the sands. Now think about this: each day Canada exports one million barrels of bitumen to the United States.

In the news, we hear that tar sands will provide oil companies with tremendous profits in the future, but there's been very little discussion about what happens next. Even hardened energy experts agree that relying on oil-soaked sand to meet North America's energy needs means that we're nearing the end of the cheap-oil era.

We know that our lifestyles must change. We know that burning fossil fuels such as oil and gas creates smog that harms our health and creates global warming. We know that global warming poses an incredible threat to humanity. We also know that there are solutions, such as creating a future based on renewable sources, increasing conservation efforts, and rethinking society so that we protect our quality of life without destroying the planet in the process. With all the money being made from the tar sands, very little of it seems to be reinvested in renewable energy that comes from wind, solar, biomass, or geothermal sources. If anything, we could be investing this money in low-carbon projects so that we won't have to pull every bit of bitumen from the ground.

When my children were younger, they'd often ask me about the bogeyman, a mythical evil spirit who'd lie in wait under their beds when the lights went out. But maybe the bogeyman isn't some scary creature. Maybe the bogeyman is simply a man in a suit trying to satisfy his shareholders, make a profit, and cozy up to federal politicians so that he can continue doing his work without having to answer for his environmental crimes.

Or maybe there's something more frightening to consider. Perhaps we're the bogeyman—when we put the short-term economic value of the tar sands above the price-less value of our environment and our health.

Rebranding won't make tar sands oil "ethical"

RIPPING A PAGE—or the cover—from fellow Conservative and former tobacco industry lobbyist Ezra Levant's book *Ethical Oil*, Canadian prime minister Stephen Harper and his environment minister, Peter Kent, have been referring to the product of the Alberta tar sands as "ethical oil."

The prime minister and Levant go back a long way. It was Levant who reluctantly stepped aside as the Alliance candidate in Calgary Southwest so that Harper could run in a by-election there in 2002. But the "ethical oil" argument they promote has holes as big as the ones in the ground around Fort McMurray.

To start, the logic is faulty. Just because a country or society is considered "ethical" does not mean everything it produces or exports is ethical. If we are going to delve into the ethics of the issue, we must look at the ethics of energy overall. That means considering the impacts of various energy systems on people and the environment. Here, the science is troubling. It shows that the Alberta tar sands contribute to about 5 per cent of Canada's greenhouse gas emissions and are the country's fastest growing source of emissions. As of early 2011, they had disturbed six hundred square kilometres of boreal forest with little or no chance of true reclamation, using enormous amounts of water and polluting the surrounding air and water.

In summer 2010, an independent, peer-reviewed scientific study showed that toxic byproducts from the tar sands extraction industry are poisoning the Athabasca River, putting downstream First Nations communities and the fish they eat at risk. Health studies show these First Nations communities already have elevated rates of rare cancers associated with exposure to such toxins.

If this is the most "ethical" source of oil we can find, we need to ask other questions about the moral purity of our intensively processed bitumen. For example, if we sell the oil to countries with poor human-rights records, like China, does that affect the product's "ethical" nature? And how "ethical" are the companies operating in the tar sands; for example, Exxon Mobil, well-known sponsor of climate-change disinformation campaigns; BP, responsible for the massive oily disaster in the Gulf of Mexico in 2010; or Petro-China? There's also the effect of greenhouse gas emissions on our children and grandchildren, which, to me, is an intergenerational crime.

In this light, wouldn't energy from technologies or sources that limit the greenhouse gas emissions that contribute to climate change and that have minimal environmental and health impacts be far more ethical than fossil fuels? And, from an economic perspective, wouldn't these more ethical technologies or fuel sources be doubly attractive to foreign buyers if they came from an "ethical" country like Canada?

The problem is, no matter what Ezra Levant and his friends in government say, oil has never been about "ethics." It has always been about money. Those who argue the case for "ethical oil" should work to ensure that our energy needs are met in a truly ethical way, now and into the future. In the end, the only truly ethical solution is to phase out oil. The black eye that tar sands oil is sporting can't be remedied with meaningless phrases such as "ethical oil."

To be seen as truly ethical when it comes to energy policy, Canada must slow down tar sands development, clean up the environmental problems, implement a national carbon tax, improve the regulatory and monitoring regime, and make sure that Canadians are reaping their fair share of the revenues. The U.S. must also look for ways to conserve energy and use cleaner sources so that it doesn't have to rely on dirty oil from the tar sands. We must start taking clean energy seriously. Rather than subsidizing the tar sands and all the fossil-fuel industry through massive tax breaks, we should be investing in energy technologies that will benefit our health, economy, and climate.

It might also help if Canada's environment minister spent more time protecting the environment rather than appeasing the oil industry and its apologists.

Fossil-fuel industry gives us cause to be skeptical

THE PRIORITY FOR people who run oil companies is to maximize profits. We know their words and actions are guided largely by a commitment to shareholders, and so we consider them in that context. Politicians, on the other hand, are supposed to represent the public interest. Supporting industry can be good for citizens, but when elected officials devote more effort to creating opportunities for industry than for the people who elect them, they lose our trust—especially when industrial growth comes at a cost to the public interest.

Given the fossil-fuel industry's record of misleading the public and endangering the environment, its support from political leaders should give us pause. The disaster in the Gulf of Mexico in 2010 when BP's *Deepwater Horizon* drilling rig exploded, killing eleven people and spewing oil into the Gulf, was a wake-up call, but it seems to be fading from memory.

We shouldn't forget this disaster, and not only because some of the millions of barrels of spilled oil is still wreaking havoc on ecosystems. The crisis was the result of a blow-out preventer failure, but the Gulf is still dotted with drilling rigs with similar devices, and most have not been properly inspected or maintained. With the *Deepwater Horizon* rig, owners were permitted to fill out their own inspection reports, which were then submitted by U.S. government regulatory agencies as being accurate.

The Gulf is also home to 27,000 abandoned oil and gas wells and 3,500 "temporarily abandoned" wells. The Associated Press reports that no one is regulating these wells to ensure they are secure and safe. Of course, cleaning up can be costly. Even though the fossil-fuel industry is the most profitable in history, and even though it continues to receive massive taxpayer-funded subsidies in the U.S., Canada, and other countries, its executives are reluctant to spend money if they don't have to. That would cut into profits.

Meanwhile, the governments of Canada and Alberta have been waging a taxpayer-funded campaign against the European Union's science-based proposal to label tar sands oil as a "high-carbon fuel." And both governments only reluctantly admitted that the tar sands are having a negative impact on the Athabasca River. Even in the face of scientific studies showing otherwise, politicians and industrialists were insisting that the tar sands were not affecting the Athabasca and that any contamination found was "naturally occurring."

Our insatiable appetite for fossil fuels has also led to concerns over hydraulic fracturing, or "fracking," whereby great amounts of water, sand, and chemicals are blasted into wells to fracture the underground shale and release natural gas. Leaks, blow-outs, water contamination, increased ozone in the atmosphere, and emissions of methane, a powerful greenhouse gas, are just some of the possible consequences of this procedure.

What this tells us, along with facts about pollution and climate change, is that we need to take a hard look at our energy use and sources. We can't expect to get reliable information from the industry; after all, its priority is to promote its own interests. And, it appears, we can't expect much better from governments, which are often led by people who are more interested in their own short-term interests, based on election cycles, than in the longer-term interests of the people who elect them.

Canada, for example, has a petro dollar. The country's economy is fuelled by high oil prices. But where will that leave Canada when the water, land, and air are polluted, when children are suffering from the effects of pollution and climate change, and when the oil has all but run out and the rest of the world has switched to cleaner energy?

The world needs a better plan than just getting as much oil, gas, and coal as fast as possible. Slower and wiser development of these resources and better ways to manage the money they generate, ensuring that the wealth is used for the good of all citizens, could help with the shift to cleaner energy. Better planning and a greater focus on renewable energy sources would benefit the health of the water, land, air, and people. It would also be much healthier for the long-term economic prosperity of the country.

Government of the people, by the corporations, for the corporations

IN 2008, ECONOMICS student Tim DeChristopher went to an auction set up by the Bush administration for the oil and gas industry. He bid $1.8 million for the right to drill on fourteen parcels of Utah wilderness, much of it near national parks, and drove up prices for other pieces of land that he bid on but didn't win. Although DeChristopher later tried to raise money online and offered to pay for the land leases, the government claimed he had no intention of paying and convicted him on two felony counts.

On July 27, 2011, he was sentenced to two years in jail and three years of probation and ordered to pay a $10,000 fine. He was escorted from the Utah courtroom in handcuffs. Now he's a criminal.

During the trial, the judge refused to allow DeChristopher to discuss his motivation. Because of that, and other reasons, his lawyers are launching an appeal. In his statement to the court before sentencing, DeChristopher said he had wanted "to stand in the way of an illegitimate auction that threatened my future." The leases were later cancelled because the Obama administration found that sufficient environmental reviews had not been conducted.

In his inspiring speech, DeChristopher also spoke eloquently about the contradictions in the law around resource extraction. He pointed out that in West Virginia, where he was raised, a state investigation found that coal-mining company Massey Energy, which often blasts away the tops of mountains to get at the coal, broke the law 62,923 times in the 10 years leading up to a disaster that killed 29 people in 2010. The company, which contributed millions of dollars to elect many appeals court judges in the state, was rarely penalized for those violations.

DeChristopher argued that his mother had tried every legal method to get coal companies to comply with the law. "She commented at hearings, wrote petitions, and filed lawsuits... to no avail," he said, adding, "I actually have great respect for the rule of law, because I see what happens when it doesn't exist, as is the case with the fossil fuel industry."

The trial, and the relatively tough sentence, hinged on the supposed damage DeChristopher caused. According to the government, oil companies were financially hurt because his actions drove the price up to an average of $125 an acre from the $12 an acre offered for land he did not bid on. That's despite the fact that companies willingly paid the higher prices and were allowed to withdraw their bids after DeChristopher was charged. And the leases were later cancelled anyway.

For his part, DeChristopher argued that "the only loss that I intended to cause was the loss of secrecy by which the government gave away public property for private profit. As I actually stated in the trial, my intent was to shine a light on a corrupt process and get the government to take a second look at how this auction was conducted."

DeChristopher's ordeal exposes the massive power of the fossil-fuel industry. Governments, including the U.S. and Canada's, often do far more to promote the interests of this industry than to protect people's rights and health. Those who violate the law and put the lives of citizens and their children and grandchildren at great risk through pollution and destructive industrial practices often get let off scot-free or receive a slap on the wrist, whereas those who use civil disobedience to challenge this imbalance are hit with the full force of the law.

Tim DeChristopher said he does not want to be a martyr; he just wants people to join him. "If the government is going to refuse to step up to that responsibility to defend a livable future, I believe that creates a moral imperative for me and other citizens. My future, and the future of everyone I care about, is being traded for short-term profits. I take that very personally."

We all should take it personally. We aren't out to shut down the fossil-fuel industry immediately. That would be impossible as well as impractical. But surely a sustainable, healthy future ought to come before a corporation's right to profit.

Oil addiction has always been messy

THE 2010 EXPLOSION on BP's *Deepwater Horizon* platform in the Gulf of Mexico and subsequent uncontrolled release of millions of litres of oil a day was a catastrophe. But why are we surprised? Oil drilling and transportation are not like brain surgery; they use brute technology to obtain and move crude oil, and oil is slopped around in this process every day. Over the years, numerous major spills have occurred on land, from drilling platforms at sea, and after collisions and breakups of ships.

Back in 1967, the *Torrey Canyon* spilled 117 million litres of crude oil off Cornwall, England. In 1976, the *Argo Merchant* dumped 29 million litres of fuel oil southeast of Nantucket Island, Massachusetts. A blowout at the offshore Ekofisk Bravo platform in 1977 released about 30 million litres of oil into the North Sea in 1977, and the *Amoco Cadiz* dumped 260 million litres off the coast of Brittany, France, in 1978. We've seen oil spilled in dozens of other collisions, blowouts, deliberate releases (in 1991, Iraq released up to 1.9 billion litres of crude oil into the Persian Gulf), and storms (in 2005, Hurricane Katrina caused the release of more than 25 million litres). In 1970, the *Arrow* spilled almost 10 million litres of oil into Chedabucto Bay in Nova Scotia, and, in 1988, the *Odyssey* dumped 159 million litres off the coast of Nova Scotia. And in 1989, the *Exxon Valdez* spilled more than 40 million litres of crude oil into the pristine waters of Prince William Sound off the Alaska coast.

Today, tens of thousands of wells operate on land and at sea, massive supertankers move huge quantities of oil across oceans, and pipelines and trucks transport oil over land. Stuff happens: earthquakes, accidents, storms, tides, icebergs, and, of course, human error.

What can we learn from the BP disaster in the Gulf of Mexico? First, there's no such thing as a "foolproof" technology because, as the computer HAL in the movie *2001: A Space Odyssey* knew, the biggest threat to a mission is a fallible, imperfect human being. We should also learn that relying so heavily on non-renewable fossil fuels for most of our energy needs carries numerous risks, from devastating spills to catastrophic climate change.

In 1979, I hosted a program called *Tankerbomb* that warned of the hazards of supertanker traffic from Alaska past the treacherous B.C. coast. A decade later, the *Exxon Valdez* spill confirmed that warning. More recently, a ferry, the *Queen of the North*, ran into Gil Island on B.C.'s north coast. Human beings are fallible, and the B.C. coast is marked by numerous rocks and reefs. That's why coastal First Nations are unanimous in their opposition to the proposed Enbridge pipeline to transport oil from the Alberta tar sands to the west coast where it would be loaded onto ships. The possibility of a tanker accident is too great a risk to their communities and fishing grounds.

Supertankers are huge, up to three hundred metres in length, and can haul enough energy to fuel a small city. It takes three kilometres and fourteen minutes for such a vessel going at full speed to stop and reverse direction. Although most newer supertankers are equipped with double hulls to reduce the threat of a spill in the event of a collision, many ships still sport single hulls.

Corporations don't focus enough on prevention nor do they consider victims of their accidents a high priority. The *Exxon Valdez* spill led to litigation by several citizens' groups, including fishermen, tour guides, and First Nations. The courts awarded them money, but the oil company appealed numerous decisions. During almost two decades of stalling, Exxon Mobil continued to earn record profits.

Supertanker accidents and the Gulf spill reveal how little attention is paid to prevention. As oil gushed from the deep-sea well in the Gulf, BP's response was pathetic. We have to plan in exquisite detail for any exigency, not play fast and loose with our claims of having everything under control. And we really must start shifting from fossil fuels to cleaner, renewable energy sources. We can all do our part by conserving energy and reducing our reliance on cars.

Oily disasters:
when will we learn?

THE 2010 GULF of Mexico oil disaster may have been the worst accidental spill in history, but another one in 1979 was almost as bad. Those of us old enough to remember may have experienced some déjà vu with the more recent disaster. On June 3, 1979, a blowout preventer failed when the Ixtoc I oil well was being drilled off the coast of Mexico. Pemex, Mexico's state oil company, owned the well, but the drilling was being done by Sedco, which later became Transocean, owner of the *Deepwater Horizon* rig where the 2010 disaster took place.

As with the 2010 crisis, the experts tried to control the 1979 spill with a number of methods, including booms, dispersants, placing a giant metal "top-kill" dome over it, and plugging it with garbage and cement. None of these techniques worked then, and they weren't successful in 2010. The Ixtoc spill lasted for more than nine months, spewing between 477 million and 795 million litres of oil that washed up on the coasts of Mexico and the U.S. It wiped out fishing along the Mexican coast for years and harmed and killed sea turtles, dolphins, birds, and other animals. In the end, the Ixtoc spill was stopped when Pemex drilled two relief wells and pumped mud and steel balls into the well. BP capped the well at the *Deepwater Horizon* after three months.

The main differences between the two spills are that no one died in the Ixtoc disaster, whereas eleven people were killed and seventeen injured in the *Deepwater Horizon* blowout, and the Ixtoc well was being drilled in forty-nine metres of water, whereas the *Deepwater Horizon* was drilling more than fifteen hundred metres deep.

It makes you wonder if we'll ever learn. In Canada, oil companies are drilling a well off the coast of Newfoundland that is even deeper than the BP well in the Gulf. Oil companies are also gearing up to drill in Arctic waters, and the

B.C. government has been putting pressure on the federal government to lift bans on drilling and oil tanker traffic off the west coast.

These spills are just a visual reminder of the damage that our fossil-fuel addiction wreaks on the environment every day. After all, if the oil weren't being spilled, it would eventually be burned, spewing carbon emissions into the atmosphere. Environmental havoc is only one reason to conserve energy and switch to cleaner energy. Security is also a crucial issue when it comes to global oil supplies. From the costly war in Iraq to the instability of some of the main oil-producing countries, we're seeing increasing problems with our reliance on this increasingly scarce energy resource.

We don't seem to be good at learning from the past. No matter what the technology or energy source, whether it's fossil fuels or nuclear power, we must be prepared for the worst-case scenario before we proceed. That's because, no matter how minimal the risk, the consequences of an accident, as we've seen from the Gulf of Mexico to Chernobyl, can be calamitous. One thing we know for certain is that relying on diminishing supplies of fossil fuels for our energy needs has serious consequences for the environment, human health, the economy, and our security. And yet governments still continue to subsidize what U.S. TV host Rachel Maddow correctly referred to in a show comparing the BP and Ixtoc oil spills as "the most profitable industry the universe has ever seen."

Let's prove that we can learn. We need to conserve energy, and we need to tell our governments that it's time to start the shift to a clean-energy economy and to keep the oil wells and tankers away from our waters.

Lubicon struggle illustrates
regulatory failures

THE FAILURE OF governments to effectively regulate the banking sector was largely responsible for the huge economic mess that hit us in 2008. Throughout the past few decades, those who were entrusted to protect the public interest have accepted as gospel—with disastrous results— the idea that governments should get out of the way and let markets self-regulate.

Unfortunately, that ideology has infiltrated our governments' thinking beyond the financial markets. At the heart of many of our most pressing environmental crises is the same belief that governments should abandon their regulatory responsibilities and allow the private sector to get on with business. (Think of the problems we've seen with weakened regulations for food and pharmaceuticals.) I was reminded of this regulatory failure in October 2008 when TransCanada Corporation, one of the world's largest pipeline companies, was granted rubber-stamp approval for a massive gas pipeline across northern Alberta. The pipeline will bring natural gas from the Canadian North over to the Fort McMurray area, where it will be used to fuel further tar sands exploitation. I say "rubber-stamp" because the company was so sure the approval was in the bag that it purchased and moved all its equipment and materials into the area before the Alberta Utilities Commission even issued its decision.

The pipeline will cross lands belonging to the Lubicon Lake Indian Nation, a small Aboriginal community that has fought for decades to have its ancestral lands in the boreal woodlands of northern Alberta recognized and protected.

Throughout that time, the Lubicon have seen their traditional way of life eroded as their lands have been leased to oil and gas companies at a breathtaking pace. They've seen more than 2,000 oil and gas well sites, 32,000 kilometres of seismic lines, and more than 2,000 kilometres of roads pushed through their forests. The Alberta government approves on average 100 new oil and gas installations in Lubicon territory each year.

The Lubicon Nation is concerned that the new pipeline will not bring long-term benefits to the community but will, instead, bring more feeder lines, more clearing, and more gas exploration and other industrial activity that will further fragment and degrade their once-rich hunting and trapping grounds in the boreal forest.

I have followed the Lubicon struggle with great interest. They were a people who lived traditionally off the land until the 1970s when they discovered that development—seismic lines, electrical lines, roads, etc.—was beginning to have an impact on their territory. They chose to fight the plans of the multinational Japanese paper company Daishowa Inc. to clear-cut their boreal forests, and, for years, they worked tirelessly to protect their land. I was honoured to help them raise money for their struggle, which ultimately proved effective in keeping the loggers at bay.

Not once but four times now the United Nations has chastised Canada for failing to resolve the Lubicon land-rights dispute, calling what is happening to the Lubicon an abuse of their human rights under international covenants. In August 2008, the UN Committee on the Elimination of Racial Discrimination wrote to Canada, saying there are "doubts as to whether the Government of Alberta and the Alberta Utilities Commission may legitimately authorize the construction of a pipeline across Lubicon territory without prior Lubicon consent." Even Amnesty International has called for a halt to the pipeline until the Lubicon concerns are met.

But none of that seems to have stopped Alberta from approving TransCanada's jumbo gas pipeline right through the heart of Lubicon lands without Lubicon approval. In the vacuum left by governments that have historically ignored their peoples' concerns, the Lubicon government is insisting on its own regulatory process that would do more than rubber-stamp increasing environmental and social disruption.

Their struggle is not new. From Haida Gwaii to Lubicon to Grassy Narrows and countless other Aboriginal communities, First Nations people have stood up against powerful industrial interests and indifferent governments. We should support the Lubicon and their actions to safeguard the idea that governments can and should regulate the economy in the public interest.

Ultimately, the Lubicon's struggle is about keeping all of us safe. The responsibility of governments to protect the environment hasn't received the same attention from politicians as the recent financial collapse, but, in the long run, environmental deregulation by governments threatens to do a lot more damage to our economies, the health of our ecosystems, and our well-being.

Is carbon capture digging us into a hole?

THE GOVERNMENTS OF Canada and Alberta are pumping billions of dollars into carbon capture and storage (CCS) as part of their climate-change plans. U.S. president Barack Obama and Canadian prime minster Stephen Harper also discussed this largely untested technology during a visit to Ottawa by the president in 2009. Projects are also being considered in Norway, Poland, Germany, and the United Kingdom. But is it a good strategy? Think of what that money could do if it were invested in energy conservation and renewable energy instead of prolonging our addiction to dirty and finite fossil fuels, especially from the tar sands.

What is CCS? People in the oil industry found that as they drained oil from wells, they could pump CO_2 back in to increase the yield. And the CO_2 appeared to stay in the ground. But we have no idea what happens to this gas. Does it form a bubble under a big rock? Is it chemically bonded to its surrounding matrix? How long will it stay down there? We don't know. We air-breathing terrestrial beings seem to have the attitude of out-of-sight, out-of-mind, so we dump our garbage into the oceans or the ground or the atmosphere, as if that were a solution.

I can't overemphasize the degree of our ignorance. Until a few years ago, scientists assumed no life existed below bedrock, but miners kept reporting that bits drilled far deeper into the ground came back contaminated. Researchers later discovered bizarre forms of life almost three kilometres below the earth's surface. The organisms are bacteria, which in some cases are embedded in rock, eking out an existence scrounging for water, energy, and nutrition. Some are thought to divide only once in a thousand years! When these organisms are brought to the surface, their DNA is unlike anything we know about bacteria above ground. Biologists have had to invent whole new phyla to describe them.

The layer of life on Earth's surface is very thin, but these single-celled organisms go down kilometres. Now, scientists believe that protoplasm living underground is more abundant than all of the elephants, trees, whales, fish, and other life above! We have no idea how important these organisms are to the subsurface web of life. Do they play a role in movement of water and nutrients, of energy from the magma? We have no idea.

I met Princeton University's Tullis Onstott, a geologist and expert on these organisms, at a lecture I gave at Princeton. I told him of the plans to pump millions of tonnes of carbon dioxide into the ground for CCS. "What effect will that have?" I asked. "I have no idea, but the methanogens should love it," he replied. "What are they?" I asked. "They absorb carbon dioxide and make methane," he responded. Methane is twenty-two times more powerful as a greenhouse gas than carbon dioxide! So, we could be pumping a greenhouse gas into the ground and ending up with a super-greenhouse gas instead. Has anyone even considered this possibility?

Remember that Paul Müller won a Nobel Prize in 1948 for his discovery in 1939 that DDT kills insects. Years after we started using it on a massive scale around the world, we learned that DDT is "biomagnified" up the food chain, harming birds, fish, and human beings. When we began to use chlorofluorocarbons, or CFCs, in spray cans, most people didn't even know there was an ozone layer, let alone that chlorine free radicals from CFCs destroy ozone. And, mark my words, we have no idea what genetically engineered organisms or nanotechnology will do. But if we humans are good at anything, it's thinking we've got a terrific idea and going for it without acknowledging the potential consequences or our own ignorance.

CCS is a simple-minded idea based on a first impression. You'd think we would have learned from the past that we shouldn't rush to apply new technologies before we know what the long-term effects will be. Carbon capture and storage may be worth studying, but the technology's potential

should not be used as an excuse for the oil and coal industries to avoid reducing their emissions and investing in
renewable energy. After all, we know that energy conservation and renewable energy will yield immediate effects of a
cleaner environment. We don't know what carbon capture
and storage will cost, when it will be commercially viable,
or what it will do, other than perhaps give us a way to keep
relying on finite and polluting sources of energy.

4

Science Holds a Mirror to Existence

As a scientist, I find all science and the scientific method fascinating. But it isn't perfect. Science has probably led to as many destructive and dangerous inventions as useful ones. It won't save us on its own. After all, science is value neutral; it won't help us with questions regarding morality or ethics. But science is still one of the best tools we have for analyzing our place in the world and our options for living well. Science is also evolving, with new fields like sustainability science and biomimicry. We've also seen a backlash against science in places like the U.S., Canada, and Australia, where scientific findings about global warming and species extinction, among other issues, often conflict with industrial and economic interests. This chapter looks at the hope science offers, as well as the challenges it faces.

New science looks at the big picture

IF WE WANT to protect an endangered animal such as the woodland caribou, we have to do more than just study the animal in isolation. We must understand how it interacts with its total environment, including its habitat and other animals, as well as humans. We must then try to determine the best possible conditions for it to live in healthy numbers and study the threats that could undermine its persistence. It's no different with humans, except that the problems we have created for ourselves—on a global scale—are even more complex.

Sometimes it seems that science is inadequate to address the myriad problems of pollution, global warming, population growth, biodiversity loss, changing ocean conditions, and so on.

Scientists don't always take a big-picture approach. Applied science, for example, is often focused on knowledge for a specific need or to solve a practical problem, such as the invention of a new technology. The science may delve into the mechanics of the technology with little regard for its social implications. Basic or "pure" science, on the other hand, is aimed at gaining an understanding of a phenomenon or process, sometimes without considering its practical application. Although both areas are valuable to society, neither alone attempts to tackle that greatest of human experiments in its entirety: our own survival.

A branch of science that has emerged over the past two decades is attempting to encompass both fundamental understanding and practical applications with a fascinating goal: to learn the degree to which humans are living in harmony with their environment and how they can continue to do so over the long term. Unlike many specialized scientific fields that might interest only a few people, this one ought to interest everyone!

Industrial society has had an enormous impact on natural ecosystems, to the point that very little of nature remains untrammelled by the human footprint. Sustainability science helps identify potential "planetary boundaries," such as the world's available "biocapacity," compared with humanity's collective "ecological footprint." In short, it helps us better understand the complex challenges we face.

The terms *sustainability* and *sustainable development* get tossed around a lot, and it's often difficult to know exactly what they mean. The most commonly cited definition is from the UN World Commission on Environment and Development, which defines sustainable development as "development that meets the needs of the present without compromising the ability of future generations to meet their own needs." Part of the difficulty is that some environmental problems are so complex and much of the science to date has addressed only fragments—dealing with one problem at a time. But the problems and their solutions are interrelated and must be looked at from a larger perspective. This is the realm of sustainability science.

We must first look at the scientific conditions necessary for a sustainable future and then look "back" to the present day, studying options for getting there. In some ways, this is opposite to the kind of forecasting that is often used in science. The U.S. National Research Council characterizes the study as a way to improve our capacity to live on the earth in a way that will "meet the needs of a much larger but stabilizing human population,... sustain the life support systems of the planet, and... substantially reduce hunger and poverty."

That's a pretty tall order. As the National Academy of Sciences points out, some issues to be resolved include improving access to clean water, developing cleaner energy and manufacturing systems, reducing the impact of pollution on human health, enhancing agricultural production and food security, creating more livable urban environments, and reducing poverty.

This branch of science is gaining respect in academic circles worldwide, but it's such an important field that it should be part of science programs in all schools. In a world that is expected to reach a population of ten billion, it's important for science to consider how we are to survive and live in harmony with the natural systems that we are a part of and therefore depend upon. It's a huge task that requires a broad vision. As more people—not just scientists—begin to understand the science and the complexity of the problems, and to design lasting solutions, we will start to see a brighter, more sustainable future.

It's time to take science seriously

LOOKING AT THE enormous changes the world has experienced over the past century, it's clear that the most powerful force shaping our lives and society was not politics or economics but science when applied by business, the pharmaceutical and medical industries, and the military. Think of the impact of antibiotics, chainsaws, nuclear weapons, computers, oral contraceptives, cars, television—the list is long. And what lies ahead? Human cloning, genetic engineering, artificial intelligence, nanotechnology, and space weapons—to say nothing of environmental issues such as climate change, deforestation, and pollution. How can any society make important decisions about these issues without being scientifically literate and informed?

Too often, the role of science in solving our social, medical, and economic problems is poorly understood because the nature of scientific research, discovery, and application is not understood. And some governments, facing economic challenges, have reduced support for science. Well, why should we support scientific research? First, good scientists make important discoveries, and to maintain a top group of scientists, we need to support and honour researchers. That can't happen when science funding becomes a political hockey puck slapped around by whichever party comes into power. We need generous long-term support for top scientists so that they can create clusters of enthusiastic, inspired researchers.

Many people believe that we must identify important areas like cancer, energy, or pollution and then direct the money to those areas so that we can look for solutions or new technologies. That is not how science works. Scientists need money to do their work, and when funding is directed at specific areas, scientists will find ways to make their work relevant to those areas. It's a game that's played to get grant money. I did it when I was an active researcher. I was interested in genetic control of cell division. When cancer-research money became available, I used the rationale that understanding the process of cell division would give us insights into the process by which cells begin to divide out of control as they become cancerous.

Scientists don't go from experiment A to B to C to D to find a cure for cancer. That's just how we write up our results or our grant proposals. Many scientists who have made important discoveries would have never qualified for research grants if the grants were specifically targeted.

Let me give you two examples from my area of training: genetics.

In the 1960s, microbial scientists puzzled over an arcane area to do with bacteria and viral infection. They found that certain viruses could infect and kill bacterial hosts whereas other bacteria seemed immune. How could the bacteria fend off viral infection? You might wonder who cares whether bacteria get sick. But out of this very esoteric work came the answer: bacteria had enzymes that recognized specific stretches of viral DNA and cut them up. These "restriction enzymes" turned out to be vital tools for genetic engineering, something that could not have been predicted when this Nobel Prize–winning work was started.

I remember as a student in the 1950s slaving over research papers by a woman studying corn. Barbara McClintock was a meticulous scientist, and we agonized over her experiments because they were so complex and elegant. She was studying genes in corn that had a peculiar property of changing locations on chromosomes. We never imagined that her work would lead to the discovery of "jumping genes" that are now a vital part of the toolbox geneticists use to modify gene behaviour. McClintock won a Nobel Prize for work that would never have qualified for grants had there been restrictions for applications.

I would urge politicians and scientists to resist rigidly restricting funding to specific research areas. Instead, they should support scientists who can be judged by their track records, by their papers and talks, in the knowledge that those scientists will have ideas, make observations, and hear about work that will be useful in some area that can't be predicted. And we must have a culture in which science is as important a part of our education as reading, writing, math, and music.

Biomimicry: nature's brilliance offers hope

SOMETIMES A NEW SCIENCE emerges that not only offers hope for our continued survival as a species but also makes obvious how little we have really learned in our relatively brief time on Earth.

In the past, it took centuries or even millennia to fully exploit a technological breakthrough, but modern technology, fuelled by cheap energy, exploded in the twentieth century. Machinery, driven by fossil fuels, has amplified our muscle power to a point where we are altering the physical, chemical, and biological features of the planet on an unprecedented scale. Some scientists have even proposed calling this the Anthropocene epoch, a time when human beings have become a geological force.

We're starting to realize, however, that although our technologies are powerful, our sense of control is often illusory; the application of brute power to bludgeon nature into apparent submission often has unexpected costs. Examples of the negative consequences of our great innovations are numerous: the pesticide DDT, splitting the atom, chlorofluorocarbons, phosphate fertilizers, and, of course, harnessing the energy of fossil fuels.

What can we learn?

To start, we must realize that we are a part of nature and that nature has a lot to teach us. I was reminded of this by an August 2010 feature article about biomimicry, entitled "Bring On Nature's Design Firm," in Toronto's NOW weekly newspaper. I've been fascinated by this subject ever since I came across the work of Janine Benyus, who is quoted in the NOW article. Benyus, an American science writer and president of the Biomimicry Institute, notes that nature has had almost four billion years to deal with the challenges humans face—how to find food and shelter, what to do with waste, how to avoid being eaten, what to do when sick, and so on. She believes we can learn from that wealth of experience.

According to the NOW article: "The biomimic asks nature how it accomplishes the different functions we humans need to carry out, like making fibres stronger than steel at low temperatures the way spiders do, out of carbohydrates with no toxins, or making solar cells that imitate the way leaves turn sunshine into energy." As the Biomimicry Institute's website points out: "The conscious emulation of life's genius is a survival strategy for the human race, a path to a sustainable future. The more our world functions like the natural world, the more likely we are to endure on this home that is ours, but not ours alone."

The institute has another website, AskNature, that demonstrates some of the wonderful potential of this science. The site allows biologists, engineers, architects, designers, and the public to share ideas and ask questions to create "biological blueprints and strategies, bio-inspired products and design sketches." And so, for example, we can learn to create self-cleaning, water-repellant surfaces by looking at the leaves of the sacred lotus, which uses nanoscale bumps to accomplish this.

Even one of the strategies of our own bodies may offer help with disasters like the Gulf oil spill: "The circulatory system of humans prevents blood loss from wounds by sending platelets to block the hole."

One of my favourites is simple: "Leaves on a forest floor create aesthetically seamless surfaces by exhibiting organized chaos." This led one of our former board members, the late Ray Anderson, founder and chair of the world's largest carpet tile manufacturer, Interface Inc., to create recyclable carpeting that can be replaced one square at a time without concern for matching the patterns because no two tiles are alike. He claimed it was the most popular brand.

Other great ideas include looking at termite mounds to learn about low-cost building ventilation, studying bamboo stems to create lightweight structural supports that don't buckle, and applying the aerodynamic efficiency of humpback whale fins to turbines, airplane wings, and underwater vehicles.

Ecosystem services are another example of how we can learn from nature and of how important it is to respect what nature has to offer. Forests store carbon, filter water, and prevent floods, yet in not taking into account the value of these services, we'll cut down the trees for the money only to end up spending much more to build filtration plants or flood-control dikes.

It will require humility to admit that we are not in control and that we depend on nature for our well-being. We have much to gain from showing respect for evolutionary solutions to our numerous challenges.

Politicians who reject science are not fit to lead

MY LIFE AS a scientist got its boost in the United States. I was attending college in Massachusetts in 1957 on a scholarship when the Soviet Union launched the first *Sputnik* satellite. The event also launched the space race between the USSR and the U.S., as the Americans started pouring money into the sciences in an attempt to catch up.

I was given funding to continue my graduate studies at the University of Chicago. On getting my PhD, I went on to work as a research associate at the Oak Ridge National Laboratory in Tennessee. Although the facility was built in 1942 as part of a top secret program to purify uranium for the Manhattan Project, its focus had shifted to basic biology by the time I arrived, and it became a centre of world-class research and international cooperation.

Times have changed. I wish I could say that we've evolved when it comes to science. But sometimes reading the news and listening to the pronouncements of politicians, especially in the United States, I'm bewildered by the rampant ignorance about science and the antipathy toward it. One example I came across was a comment by the governor of Maine, Paul LePage, about bisphenol A, or BPA, which is used mainly in plastic containers and toys. Health Canada declared BPA a toxic chemical because of its links to breast cancer, developmental problems in children, prostate disease, and fertility issues.

In response to calls for his state to restrict BPA use, LePage said, "There hasn't been any science that identifies that there is a problem. The only thing that I've heard is if you take a plastic bottle and put it in the microwave and you heat it up, it gives off a chemical similar to estrogen. So the worst case is some women may have little beards."

It's a profoundly ignorant statement for anyone to make, let alone a state governor, but it's only the tip of the iceberg. Science is taking a beating in the U.S., and a similar phenomenon is starting to occur in Canada, though not to as great an extent.

Far more dangerous are attempts by U.S. politicians to attack the overwhelming scientific evidence that human activity is causing catastrophic climate change. Despite countless studies by scientists from around the world and agreement among 98 per cent of the world's climate scientists and most of the world's scientific academies and societies that greenhouse gas emissions are causing the earth's average temperature to rise, not to mention the facts staring us in the face—increased frequency of extreme weather conditions, rising sea levels, melting ice caps and glaciers—some politicians in the U.S. continue to reject the science and argue that we must proceed with business as usual.

Virginia's Republican attorney general, Kenneth Cuccinelli, has spent taxpayer dollars attacking climate scientists at the University of Virginia and tried to sue the U.S. Environmental Protection Agency over its ruling that carbon dioxide and other global warming gases are a threat to human health and welfare. Many Republicans, some of whom also reject the science of evolution and believe the earth was created six thousand years ago and that humans and dinosaurs walked together, have followed his lead.

As for the so-called Climategate brouhaha (where more than one thousand emails between climate scientists at the University of East Anglia were stolen or leaked by hackers), a fifth investigation, this time led by Republicans in response to a request from one of their own, Senator James Inhofe of Oklahoma, again found no "evidence to question the ethics of our scientists or raise doubts about [the National Oceanic and Atmospheric Administration's] understanding of climate change science."

Efforts in the U.S. to sow confusion about climate science appear to be having an effect: according to a 2011 poll, only 58 per cent of U.S. citizens believe in the science behind climate change, compared with 80 per cent of Canadians. However, the situation in Canada isn't much better. Canada's government has cut funding for climate research, rejected or ignored scientific studies showing environmental damage from the tar sands, and been accused of "muzzling" scientists.

Science isn't perfect, and it can be used for destructive as well as beneficial purposes. But it's the best tool we have for analyzing and understanding our world and the impact of our actions on the environment of which we are a part. If our leaders reject science, we really are in trouble.

Sometimes it does take a rocket scientist... to take on Hollywood

HEDY LAMARR WAS once regarded as the most beautiful woman in Hollywood. In 1933, she scandalously appeared nude in a Czech film called *Ecstasy*, which brought her to the attention of U.S. movie moguls. Through the 1930s, '40s, and '50s, she starred in some of Hollywood's biggest hits alongside leading male celluloid idols like Spencer Tracy and Clark Gable. She was also a part-time rocket scientist. In fact, we have her to thank for some of the technology used in cellphones and the Internet.

In 1940, Lamarr and avant-garde music composer George Antheil devised and patented a communications system based on "frequency hopping" for use in radio-guided torpedoes. Their invention was inspired by player piano rolls—spools of paper with holes that "told" automatic pianos which notes to play. Frequency hopping is now used in much of our wireless communications technology. Because the invention was long classified as top secret, her contribution wasn't recognized for years, and many people were surprised to learn that a glamorous star could also have a brilliant scientific mind.

Why should we be surprised? Are you surprised to learn that, during high school, Oscar winner Natalie Portman was a straight-A student and semifinalist in the rigorous

Intel Science Talent Search for her investigation into an environmentally friendly way to convert waste into energy and that she went on to study neuroscience and the evolution of the mind at Harvard? During her studies, she still found time to act in a string of major movies.

According to a February 2011 article in the *New York Times*, Portman and Lamarr are not alone. Danica McKellar had roles in shows including *The Wonder Years, The West Wing*, and *NYPD Blue*. As a math student at the University of California, Los Angeles, she also helped come up with a mathematical theorem that was named after her and her collaborators. Mayim Bialik, who stars as neurobiologist Amy Farrah Fowler in the popular TV show *The Big Bang Theory*, really is a neurobiologist, with a PhD from UCLA. She also played the lead role in the '90s TV show *Blossom*.

These examples aren't about overachieving stars. Rather, they're a way of pointing out that science isn't just for nerds—and it isn't just for guys. But it also says something about Western society's obsession with celebrity and its lack of interest in science. We pay far more attention to these people for their movie roles and stardom than for their scientific and academic accomplishments.

Contrary to what the endless columns in newspapers and magazines or minutes of broadcast time would lead you to believe, celebrity, sports, business, and politics are not the most important issues. The reality is that the most powerful force shaping our lives today is science, whether it's in industry, medicine, or the military. We cannot control the ideas and inventions unleashed by science if we, as a society, are scientifically illiterate. We elect our politicians to represent us and lead us into the future, and they must make decisions to deal with climate change, overpopulation, endocrine disrupters, stem cells, cloning, genetically modified organisms, pollution, deforestation, and a host of other issues that require some understanding of science.

The lesson we should take from people like Portman, who also created an environmental video in her childhood, is that it's fine to be entertained and to entertain, but that shouldn't preclude us from taking an interest in the world around us and in the science that shapes so much of our place in that world and helps us to understand it.

We can't all be scientists, just as we can't all be movie stars, but we can take the time to learn more about science and its application in understanding and solving some of the challenges we face in the modern world. I've had only one small role in a short fictional film, and, I can tell you, it's tedious work. I'd much rather be a scientist. But I'm glad there are movie stars who are interested in science. With so many poor role models in the movie business and in politics, it's refreshing to see some who are setting good examples.

5

Is the Economy... Stupid?

OUR CURRENT ECONOMIC paradigm has served its purpose: to get goods and services efficiently to ever-expanding human populations. But along the way we've lost sight of what an economy is supposed to do, and we've lost sight of the fact that an economic system is a human invention that can be modified, improved, or changed to suit our needs, as it often has—sometimes gradually, as we've seen in North America over the past century, and sometimes through sudden upheaval, as we saw with the collapse of the Soviet Union. It's absurd that we still rely on a recently devised economic system based on endless growth when we live on a finite planet. It's also absurd that things many of us would consider to be negative, such as wars, natural disasters, and accidents, can actually have positive effects on the economy by generating jobs and production. Politicians and business people often elevate the economy to a higher place than the environment. But without all the goods and services that the natural environment provides for us, we wouldn't even be here to talk about the economy. It's time to find better ways to get the economy to work for us, rather than the other way around.

It's time for a new economic paradigm

I'VE HEARD ECONOMISTS boast that their discipline is based on a fundamental human impulse: selfishness. They claim that we act first out of self-interest. I can agree, depending on how we define *self*. To some, "self" extends beyond the individual person to include immediate family. Others might include community, an ecosystem, or all other species. I list *ecosystem* and *other species* deliberately because we have become a narcissistic, self-indulgent species. We believe we are at the centre of the world, and everything around us is an "opportunity" or "resource" to exploit. Our needs or demands trump all other possibilities. This is an anthropocentric view of life.

Thus, when faced with a choice of logging or conserving a forest, we focus on the potential economic benefits of logging or not logging. When the economy experiences a downturn, we demand that nature pay for it. We relax pollution standards, increase logging or fishing above sustainable levels, or (as the federal government has decreed) lift the requirement of environmental assessments for new projects.

A fundamentally different perspective on our place in the world is called "biocentrism." In this view, life's diversity encompasses everything, and we humans are a part of it, ultimately deriving everything we need from it. Viewed this way, our well-being, indeed our survival, depends on the health and well-being of the natural world. I believe this view better reflects reality.

The most pernicious aspect of our anthropocentrism has been the elevation of economics to the highest priority. We act as if the economy is some kind of natural force that we must all placate or serve in every way possible. But some things, like gravity, the speed of light, entropy, and the first and second laws of thermodynamics, are forces of nature. There's nothing we can do about them except live within the boundaries they delineate. But the economy, the market, currency—we created these entities, and if they fail, we should look beyond trying to get them back up and running the way they were. We should fix them or toss them out and replace them.

When economists and politicians met in Bretton Woods, New Hampshire, in 1944, they faced a world in which war had devastated countrysides, cities, and economies. So they tried to devise solutions. They pegged currency to the American greenback and looked to the (terrible) twins, the International Monetary Fund and the World Bank, to get economies going again. The postwar era saw amazing recovery in Europe and Japan, as well as a roaring U.S. economy based on supplying a cornucopia of consumer goods. But the economic system that was created in Bretton Woods is fundamentally flawed because it is disconnected from the biosphere, the zone of air, water, and land in which we live. We cannot afford to ignore these flaws any longer. Let's take a look at them.

Flaw 1: Beyond its obvious value as the source of raw materials like fish, lumber, and food, nature performs all kinds of "services" that allow us to survive and flourish. Nature creates topsoil, the thin skin that supports all agriculture. Nature removes carbon dioxide from the atmosphere and returns oxygen. Nature takes nitrogen from the air and fixes it to enrich soil. Nature filters water as it percolates through soil. Nature transforms sunlight into molecules that we need for energy in our bodies. Nature degrades the carcasses of dead plants and animals and disperses the atoms and molecules back into the biosphere. Nature pollinates flowering plants.

I could go on, but I think you catch my drift. We cannot duplicate what nature does around the clock, but we dismiss those services as "externalities" in our economy.

Flaw 2: To compound the problem, economists believe that because there are no limits to human creativity, there need be no limits to the economy. But the economy depends on having healthy people, and health depends on nature's services, which are ignored in economic calculations. Our home is the biosphere, the thin layer of air, water, and land where all life exists. And that's it; it can't expand. We are witnessing the collision of the economic imperative to grow indefinitely with the finite services that nature performs. It's time to get our perspective and priorities right. Biocentrism is a good place to start.

The first Bretton Woods conference helped us devise solutions for the challenges of the time. Now we have new challenges for new times. It's time for a Bretton Woods II.

The behemoth that wouldn't stop growing

HAVE YOU NOTICED that we describe the market and the economy as if they were living entities? The market is showing signs of stress. The economy is healthy. The economy is on life support. Sometimes, we act as if the economy is larger than life. In the past, people trembled in fear of dragons, demons, gods, and monsters, sacrificing anything—virgins, money, newborn babies—to appease them. We know now that those fears were superstitious imaginings, but we have replaced them with a new behemoth: the economy.

Even stranger, economists believe this behemoth can grow forever. Indeed, the measure of how well a government or corporation is doing is its record of economic growth. But our home—the biosphere—is finite and fixed. It can't grow. And nothing within such a world can grow indefinitely. In focusing on constant growth, we fail to ask the important questions. What is an economy for? Am I happier with all the stuff it supplies? How much is enough?

A timely book by York University environmental economist Peter Victor, *Managing Without Growth: Slower by Design, Not Disaster*, addresses the absurdity of an economic system based on endless growth. Victor also shows that the concept of growth as an indispensable feature of economics is a recent phenomenon.

The economy is not a force of nature or some kind of immutable, infallible entity. We created it, and when problems occur, it makes no sense to simply shovel more money into it to keep it going. Because it's a human invention, an economy is something we should be able to fix or replace with something better.

Our continuing economic crisis provides an opportunity to re-examine our priorities. For decades, scientists and environmentalists have been alarmed at global environmental degradation. Today, the oceans are depleted of fish, and "dead zones," immense islands of plastic, and acidification from dissolving carbon dioxide are having untold effects. We have altered the chemistry of the atmosphere with our emissions, causing the planet to heat up, and we have cleared land of forests, along with hundreds of thousands of species. Using air, water, and soil as dumps for our industrial wastes, we have poisoned ourselves.

For the first time in four billion years of life on Earth, one species has become so powerful and plentiful that it is altering the physical, chemical, and biological features of the planet on a geological scale. And so we have to ask, "What is the collective impact of everyone in the world?" We've never had to ask that question before, and it's difficult to answer. Even when we do contemplate our global effects, we have no mechanism for responding as one species to the crises.

Driving much of this destructive activity is the economy itself. Years ago, during a heated debate about clear-cutting, a forestry company CEO yelled at me, "Listen, Suzuki, are tree huggers like you willing to pay to protect those trees? Because if you're not, they don't have any value until someone cuts them down!" I was dumbstruck with the realization that in our economic system, he was correct. You see, as long as that forest is intact, the plants photosynthesize and remove carbon dioxide from the air while putting oxygen back—not a bad service for animals like us that depend on clean air. But economists dismiss this as an "externality." What they mean is that photosynthesis is not relevant to the economic system they've created!

Tree roots cling to the soil so that when it rains the soil doesn't erode into the river and clog the salmon-spawning gravels: another externality to economists. The trees pump hundreds of thousands of litres of water out of the soil, transpiring it into the air and modulating weather and climate—an externality. The forest provides habitat for countless species of bacteria, fungi, insects, mammals, amphibians, and birds—externality. So all the things an intact ecosystem does to keep the planet vibrant and healthy for animals like us are simply ignored in our economy. No wonder futurist Hazel Henderson describes conventional economics as "a form of brain damage."

Nature's services keep the planet habitable for animals like us and must become an integral component of a new economic structure. We must let go of this suicidal focus on endless, mindless growth.

If I had four trillion dollars

MANY OF YOU are working to recycle, reduce energy consumption, and improve the world for your families and neighbours. The collective impact of these many small efforts is making a big difference.

Just think what you could do with $4.1 trillion!

That's how much the U.S. and 17 Western European countries spent to bail out financial institutions involved in an economic crisis that began in the U.S. and soon reverberated around the world. (The final amount was likely a lot more. It's difficult to fathom such a large number, but consider that 1 trillion seconds is about 32,000 years!) To top it off, most of the details are secret; we don't really know what the money is being used for—though it probably didn't stop your retirement savings funds from plummeting.

The effect on people in developing nations is even worse. Most of them didn't have savings to begin with, and the economic crisis, coupled with the effects of the climate crisis—including drought and food shortages—is causing more of our human family to suffer from extreme poverty and joblessness.

Just think what they could do with $4.1 trillion!

A 2008 report from the Institute for Policy Studies (IPS), "Skewed Priorities: How the Bailouts Dwarf Other Global Crisis Spending," points out that the amount is forty times what the U.S. and Europe are spending in developing nations on programs to deal with poverty ($90.7 billion) and climate change ($13.1 billion, none of it from the U.S.). In fact, the U.S. spent far more to bail out insurance firm AIG ($152.5 billion) than all the countries together spent on developmental aid in 2007. And what did the AIG executives do after getting the taxpayer-funded bailout? They celebrated, with a $440,000 trip to a luxury spa resort. The cost of the trip was about what the U.S. spent in 2007 on food aid to Lebanon, "a country struggling to recover from conflict," according to the IPS.

If we think we needn't worry about what happens to developing nations because it isn't affecting us, we should remind ourselves that just as everything in nature is connected, so is everything in our global economic and political systems. Increased international job competition and reduced export opportunities are just two of the smaller impacts mentioned in the IPS report. But the worst meltdown isn't of the global economy. Another report, "Climate Safety," from the Public Interest Research Centre, shows that the Arctic's late-summer ice is melting much faster than scientists previously predicted and may soon disappear. The cascading consequences of such an event could be catastrophic.

Just think what we could do with $4.1 trillion!

Instead of giving companies these huge sums of money so that they can continue business as usual, buying and selling, merging, and paying their executives obscene salaries and bonuses, we could put it toward renewable energy, sustainable urban planning, and research into ways to lessen the impact of climate change—things that really would stimulate economies. But the focus continues to remain on the false dichotomy of economy versus environment.

Eminent economist Lord Stern said that meeting the challenge of climate change could cost about 1 per cent of annual GDP, but doing nothing could destroy the global economy. It seems there's only one thing we can do, and it won't cost $4.1 trillion.

As citizens, we can and must do everything possible to keep our finite world alive and healthy. Along with the small but important changes we are making in our own lives, we must also call on our leaders to stop downplaying the unequivocal science that tells us that failing to quickly address the climate crisis will make the economic crisis seem like a minor blip in history.

We could tell them where to put that $4.1 trillion!

Will saving a forest save us money?

HOW MUCH IS a forest worth? And how do we calculate that value? Do we simply count the trees and figure out how much we could get for them if we were to cut them down and turn them into logs, lumber, and pulp and paper?

That's been the traditional approach, but it hasn't served us well. A forest is much more than the timber it holds. A forest provides habitat for wildlife, recreational opportunities for hikers and hunters, a place for quiet contemplation, and filtration and storage of drinking water. And because forests absorb carbon dioxide from the atmosphere and store it in their trees and soils, they are a critical "hedge" against global warming.

When we take into account all of the ecological benefits, or services, a forest provides, we have to re-evaluate the decisions we make about how we manage them. Clear-cutting an old-growth forest may provide temporary jobs and profits, as well as two-by-fours to build homes and furniture, but if it also results in the release of carbon stored in the trees and soil, thus contributing to global warming, or if it wipes out the habitat of an animal that is crucial to the natural order, then the short-term gains may not be worthwhile.

Two reports by the David Suzuki Foundation and its allies illustrate the idea of taking into account the full suite of values that a forest represents, or its "natural capital," when making decisions about resource management. "Dollars and Sense: The Economic Rationale to Protect the Spotted Owl Habitat in British Columbia" and "The Real Wealth of the Mackenzie Region: Assessing the Natural Capital Values of a Northern Boreal Ecosystem" both argue for a more holistic approach to managing our natural ecosystems.

For a long time, we've considered only the immediate market value of resources when making decisions about forest use. In doing so, we've ignored the enormous value of the ecosystem services that are critical to biodiversity, human health, and community well-being. Although it's not easy to put a dollar value on things such as carbon sequestration and storage, water filtration, clean-water availability, and species diversity, it's foolish to leave them out of the equation.

For "Dollars and Sense," researchers looked not just at the value of timber in old-growth forests in British Columbia inhabited by the endangered spotted owl but also at the value of recreational uses and non-timber forest products, and the role the forests play in storing carbon. They concluded that "in seventy-two of eighty-one scenarios, increased forest conservation yields better economic returns than does status quo logging and limited conservation." The Mackenzie report concludes that the non-market value of that region is eleven times greater than the market value. The researchers estimate that the market value, based on gross domestic product, is $41.9 billion a year, whereas the non-market value, based on seventeen ecosystem services, is $483.8 billion.

The outcome in the Mackenzie region has been positive. Under the Northwest Territories Protected Area Strategy—a collaborative effort between the governments of Canada and the Northwest Territories, First Nations, conservation groups, and industry—the federal government announced plans to protect 10.1 million hectares of northern boreal forest. The goal is to create a culturally and ecologically representative network of protected areas, ensuring that communities benefit from both conservation and development. The areas will be protected from industrial development, including oil and gas exploration and diamond and uranium mining.

The spotted owl habitat hasn't fared as well. The B.C. government has not announced any plans to increase levels of protection for these areas. But it's not just about saving the spotted owl, as important as that is. It's about finding a balance and ensuring that we derive the greatest benefit for all from our forestlands.

Taking into account all the values of a forest doesn't mean an end to logging and mining; it just means finding better ways to manage all of our activities in these ecosystems—and it means putting a value on the very real services they provide. If we don't address the serious problems of global warming and biodiversity loss, as well as issues such as access to clean air and water, we may well join the spotted owl on the endangered list.

Accounting for nature's goods and services

BLUEBERRIES HAVE BECOME the biggest fruit crop in British Columbia, bringing in close to $100 million in annual sales. That's a lot of money for farmers, pickers, packagers, distributors, and grocery stores. But the essential service provided by one of the hardest workers in the blueberry industry rarely makes it into the account ledgers.

If it weren't for the wild bees that pollinate the blueberry fields in the Fraser Valley, near Vancouver, and elsewhere, berry yields would collapse. In fact, declines in honeybees and other agricultural pollinators as a result of habitat loss, pesticide use, and other human activities mean that farmers are now paying to replace this critical natural service. In many areas of the U.S. and Canada, farmers are trucking beehives onto their farms to ensure that the once-free pollination services their crops depend on continue.

This is just one illustration of the value of the services provided by nature, and of the costs of poor ecological management. Other examples of the benefits nature provides are numerous. Our forests, for example, ensure that steep slopes remain stable, that flood risks are lower, and that drinking water in our cities comes out of our taps filtered and clean.

We'd do well to take a closer look at the real value of the benefits nature provides. Protecting nature can actually result in cost savings for governments, since it can act as an important buffer against the full impacts of economic downturns. That's partly because the costs to replace natural services that have been degraded or lost due to mismanagement are prohibitively high.

Recognition of the irreplaceable value of ecosystem services and the impact of human development on them is emerging nationally and globally. For instance, the United

Nations Millennium Ecosystem Assessment concluded that about 60 per cent of the world's ecosystem services are being used at an unsustainable rate. In Canada, the U.S., Brazil, the United Kingdom, Australia, and elsewhere, the establishment of "greenbelts" of protected farmland, forests, watersheds, wetlands, and other green spaces around cities has helped to protect essential ecosystem services. The benefits provided by southern Ontario's greenbelt alone have been conservatively estimated at $2.6 billion annually.

But conventional economic thinking ignores the value of nature's services. Thus, the ecological cost of an apple shipped from New Zealand to North America is not properly included in the pricing when we buy that apple for a dollar. In the same way, when we throw away a cellphone or laptop, the cost of that waste is not accounted for. We need a new accounting system that includes the value of nature's services and the costs of our waste and pollution.

As for the current economic crisis, shovelling more money at failing economic institutions will, at best, only buy us time until the real meltdown hits. A new global economy is emerging from this crisis, and it's a green economy.

Investing in programs to maintain, enhance, and restore ecosystem services that natural areas provide is an effective cost-saving measure and an important element of any green economy. For a fraction of the cost of the massive economic bailouts, we could protect the natural areas that provide these services and see greater economic benefits—not to mention improved health and community well-being. For example, New York City invested in a program of watershed protection through land purchase, pollution control, and conservation easements and in doing so saved billions of dollars that would have been otherwise needed for new infrastructure to ensure clean drinking water.

A few small efforts by governments could go a long way to ensuring that we continue to receive these benefits from nature and that we don't incur the enormous costs of replacing them if nature is degraded—if they can even be replaced. Governments should fund stewardship and other incentive programs that reward farmers for conservation efforts. They should also put more money into wildlife areas and migratory bird sanctuaries and provide tax incentives for donations that help preserve ecologically significant lands.

If we were to include natural services and the environmental costs of our waste and pollution in our economic accounting, we'd have a more realistic economic system. And we'd see that the environment and the economy are intertwined. Caring for one is the solution to problems facing the other.

Harming the environment is bad for the economy

WE OFTEN POINT out that *ecology* and *economy* have the same root, from the Greek *oikos*, meaning "home." Ecology is the study of home, and economics is its management. But many people still insist on treating them as two separate, often incompatible, processes.

At its most absurd, the argument is that we simply can't afford to protect the environment—that the costs will be so high as to ruin the economy. But if you don't take care of your home, it will eventually become uninhabitable, and where's the economic justification for that? Others argue that the economic advantages of some activities outweigh the environmental disadvantages. This, too, is an absurd argument. A June 2009 article on the website Grist.org,

"Screwing Up Environment Not So Great for Economy, Studies Find," pointed to a number of studies and articles showing that many of these activities are not even beneficial from an economic standpoint.

Take coal mining. Research from West Virginia University found that "coal mining costs Appalachians five times more in early deaths as the industry provides to the region in jobs, taxes, and other economic benefits." And, according to Grist, the Mountain Association for Community Economic Development found that "the coal industry takes $115 million more from Kentucky's state government annually in services and programs than it contributes in taxes." The website also referred to a peer-reviewed study in the journal *Science* that concluded that logging in Brazil's rainforests offered only short-term gains in income, life expectancy, and literacy, but that the gains disappear over the long term, "leaving deforested municipalities just as poor as those that preserved their forests."

Yet another study found that all the big three U.S. automakers need to do to become profitable and to compete with Japanese car manufacturers is to meet new government-mandated fuel economy standards. Studies have also shown that bear watching can be more profitable than bear hunting, and the Grist article likewise notes that whale watching is more profitable than killing whales.

Often the problem is not so much with resource exploitation itself but rather with the way we exploit our resources and the reasons for the exploitation. With CEOs looking at quarterly results and politicians looking at three- or four-year terms of office, the incentives for long-range thinking are not always clear.

One of the most horrendous examples of this worm's-eye view can be seen in Canada's tar sands. As author Andrew

Nikiforuk argues in his award-winning book *Tar Sands: Dirty Oil and the Future of a Continent*, this resource could be used wisely to "fund Canada's transition to a low-carbon economy." Instead, industrial interests and the Alberta and federal governments are hell-bent on full-scale liquidation. We will end up with some short-term profits and a seemingly healthy economy in exchange for massive environmental damage and the rapid depletion of a resource that may still be necessary for some time to come—along with the resulting negative economic consequences.

Part of the problem lies in the real reason for much of our resource exploitation and industrial activity. A lot of it is done not out of necessity but out of a desire of a relatively small number of people to make lots of money quickly. And when the money is rolling in and jobs are being created, the politicians who foster the activities look good.

We may need fossil fuels, at least for now, but do we really need them so that one or two people can propel themselves to the grocery store in a massive suv made from tonnes of metal? We also see, not surprisingly, that the dinosaurs of the fossil-fuel and other industries will go to great lengths to protect their interests. If that means spreading misinformation and outright lies about the consequences of their industries, well, so be it.

Even though the scientific proof for human-caused global warming is undeniable, the coal and oil industries are funding massive campaigns to cast doubt on the science and politicians are implying that the world's scientists are involved in some sinister plot—so that we can continue to rely on diminishing supplies of polluting fuels instead of creating jobs and wealth through a greener economy that may save us from catastrophe.

We need only look at political discourse in the United States leading up to the 2012 presidential election to see that the people standing in the way of progress on the environment are often just as ignorant about the economy.

Carbon offsets: a tool in the fight against global warming

THE SCIENCE IS CLEAR: human-caused global warming is a reality. Now it's time to focus on solutions. We need strong leadership from our governments in setting firm greenhouse gas reduction targets, and we need to look at a range of policies and practices. There is no legitimate argument about whether the problem exists, but there is still some debate about the best ways to tackle it.

Take carbon offsets. Some people compare them to indulgences granted by the church allowing sinners to avoid punishment for some transgressions. Others argue that offsets can be one of many legitimate tools used to tackle climate change and that high-quality carbon offsets can result in real reductions in greenhouse gas emissions.

Carbon offsets are becoming an increasingly popular way for individuals, businesses, and even governments to reduce their impact on the environment. The "voluntary" carbon market, made up of all these purchases of carbon offsets, increased in value globally from $305 million in 2007 to $460 million in 2008. If you add in the offsets that are used in national and international regulatory programs, such as the Kyoto Protocol and European Union Emissions Trading System, the total carbon market now approaches $139 billion a year.

So carbon offsets are here to stay. But what are they? Well, a carbon offset is a credit for a reduction in greenhouse gas emissions generated by one project, such as a solar-power installation, that can be used to cancel out the emissions from another source. Carbon offsets are typically measured in tonnes of CO_2 or their equivalent. Those who buy offsets are essentially investing in other projects that reduce emissions on their behalf, either because they are unable to do so themselves or because it is too expensive to make their own reductions.

But not all carbon offsets are created equal. Because the market is new and largely unregulated, some offsets are unlikely to have any benefit for the climate. This is one reason why carbon offsets have gotten a bad rap. So, what makes a good offset? Opinions vary on some of the finer points, but most experts agree that several conditions are necessary. Good offsets are "additional"; that is, they result in greenhouse gas reductions that wouldn't have otherwise occurred without the incentive of carbon offsets. For example, if a company is required by regulation to install technology to reduce emissions from its factory, the resulting emission reductions should not be sold as offsets.

A good carbon offset should also result in "permanent" reductions in greenhouse gas emissions. This is one reason why some organizations recommend against using tree planting to generate offsets. Although trees have many benefits for the environment, they make risky carbon offsets because they are susceptible to fire, logging, and insect infestation—any one of which can release the stored carbon back into the atmosphere and render the offset worthless. Good carbon offsets should also be verified by qualified auditors to ensure that the reductions have actually taken place.

Carbon offsets that are real, additional, and permanent can have a direct, positive impact on the climate. And they can create some other important benefits. They provide money for much-needed renewable-energy and energy-efficiency projects, which can help move society away from fossil fuels and toward a clean-energy economy. Buying carbon offsets can also help to deal with emissions that aren't currently covered by government regulations, such as international air travel. Carbon offsets can also put a value on carbon and help to educate businesses and consumers about the climate impact of their daily decisions and where they should target their own reduction efforts.

People should do everything they can to reduce their greenhouse gas emissions, but when that isn't possible or feasible, buying high-quality offsets at least ensures that an equivalent amount of reductions is made elsewhere.

Carbon offsets alone won't solve climate change. We still need to find ways to make deep reductions in our own emissions. But the problem of climate change is so massive that it requires a range of solutions, and offsets can be part of that.

Let's clear the air on carbon taxes

I ADMIT WE AREN'T 100 per cent sure that human activity is causing global warming. So let's all go home in our SUVs and forget about fossil-fuel consumption. Come to think of it, we aren't sure that our houses will be robbed, flooded, or burned to the ground, so let's cancel our home insurance while we're at it.

After all, the majority of the world's climate scientists will admit to being only more than 90 per cent certain that our carbon emissions are causing global warming on such a scale that we face global catastrophe if we fail to change our ways. If nine out of ten doctors said your child needed an immediate operation, would you wait until all ten agreed? James Hansen, a leading climate expert who raised the alarm about global warming to the U.S. Congress in the late 1980s, says he's 99 per cent sure, but that's still not 100 per cent, so why should we pay more by way of a carbon tax to address a problem that may not exist?

True, a report prepared by M.K. Jaccard and Associates for the David Suzuki Foundation, titled "Pricing Carbon: Saving Green," argued persuasively that a carbon tax is an effective tool for bringing emissions down, and governments, scientists, and economists around the world agree— but what if they're wrong? Never mind that countries such as Sweden, which implemented a carbon tax in 1991, have proven that such measures are effective and that they actually produce economic benefits; why should we change if we don't have to? Rising gas prices due to global market forces are already hitting us hard enough; why should we add to the misery?

Consider this: if the industry shills and their followers are right and global warming is not the threat we think it is, and we act anyway, the oil will still be there for future use and we'll also have cleaner air and greater innovation in green technologies—along with stronger economies. If the majority of the world's climate scientists are right and we fail to act, we face ecological, social, and economic catastrophe on a scale beyond anything we can imagine.

Consider also that carbon taxes are often tax shifts. The money collected from individuals, businesses, and industry can be returned in the form of cuts to personal and business taxes. Often, the increases in gas prices with a carbon tax are minuscule compared with market increases, and the tax can help us move away from continued reliance on increasingly scarce and costly fossil fuels. Whether it's called a tax shift, a revenue-neutral tax, or a new tax, it will get people worked up. No one likes taxes, but we like roads and schools and hospitals and police services, so we pay them. We also pay fees to put garbage into landfills, so why are we so concerned about having to pay to put garbage into the air?

Politicians have two powerful instruments to influence behaviour: regulation and taxation. In the mindless mantra of anti-taxation groups, taxes are bad and we should always cut and never increase them. The ludicrous aspect is that while resisting even a small tax hike, these groups are silent about the enormous taxpayer subsidies to fossil-fuel and related industries that make windfall profits.

Together with measures such as a cap-and-trade program, a carbon tax can use money from industries that are not energy efficient to create economic benefits and incentives for those that are wiser in their energy use. The income generated by a carbon tax can be used to cut income taxes, build more public transit, upgrade trains, develop renewable-energy sources, and retrofit homes and buildings with energy-efficient technology.

For more than twenty years, scientists have warned of the need for urgent action to reduce greenhouse gas emissions. Leading economists have shown that the cost to bring emissions down will be about 1 per cent of GDP annually, whereas the costs incurred if we don't reduce emissions could be economically catastrophic.

When politicians, business people, and citizens show leadership by proposing or implementing solutions to the very real problems facing the planet (yes, more than 90 per cent certain is as real as it gets in science), they deserve our support.

Climate change is a symptom
of economic madness

POLITICIANS OFTEN USE the economy as an excuse to ignore international obligations to combat climate change and to rebuff serious discussion about the need to reduce greenhouse gas emissions, develop renewable energy, and create green jobs.

Raising the spectre of economic disaster is a convenient way to downplay or ignore other issues, but global ecological degradation has enormous economic implications. In his groundbreaking analysis of the economics of climate change, former World Bank chief economist Lord Stern concluded that taking action to keep heat-trapping greenhouse gas emissions below levels that would cause catastrophic climate change could require investment of 2 to 3 per cent of annual global GDP. That's a huge amount of money, but such a massive investment would create jobs and move us to a sustainable and healthy energy future. Lord Stern also pointed out that failing to bring down greenhouse gas emissions will destroy the economy, costing more than the First and Second World Wars combined!

How can anyone who claims to be concerned about the economy ignore this?

The challenges we face are far more profound than just economic collapse. They threaten the very existence of civilization. The environmental crisis is not just about greenhouse gas emissions, pollution, disappearing forests, or vanishing species. It's about whether the biosphere can continue to support top predators, and no species is higher up the food chain than humans.

In a debate in the U.K.'s *Guardian* newspaper between George Monbiot and Paul Kingsnorth (August 18, 2009), both well-known writers and environmentalists, Kingsnorth refers to a set of graphs with the same horizontal axis measuring time from 1750 to 2000. The graphs measure "population levels, CO_2 concentration in the atmosphere, exploitation of fisheries, destruction of tropical forests, paper consumption, number of motor vehicles, water use, the rate of species extinction, and the totality of the human economy's gross domestic product."

What's amazing is that although they measure such disparate factors, the graphs' curves are almost identical: "A line begins on the left of the page, rising gradually as it moves to the right. Then, in the last inch or so—around 1950—it veers steeply upwards."

We are familiar with these curves, especially for population. Try this: take a piece of paper and draw a horizontal line representing time, ranging from 150,000 years ago (when our species appeared on Earth) to the present. For more than 99 per cent of its length, the curve is virtually flat, rising imperceptibly until finally reaching a billion in the last pencil-width of time around 1830. Then the curve leaps straight up off the page to 7 billion now. Nothing can rise so steeply without hitting limits, resulting in rapid collapse.

What was Kingsnorth's conclusion? "The root cause of all these trends is the same: a rapacious human economy bringing the world swiftly to the brink of chaos."

He argues that many of us, including "much of the mainstream environmental movement," ignore this reality because we "are still wedded to a vision of the future as an upgraded version of the present. We still believe in 'progress,' as lazily defined by western liberalism." Although I lean toward Monbiot's somewhat more optimistic arguments in the debate, I fear Kingsnorth makes some undeniable points.

"Climate change is teetering on the point of no return while our leaders bang the drum for more growth," Kingsnorth argues. "The economic system we rely upon cannot be tamed without collapsing, for it relies upon that growth to function."

We cannot keep fooling ourselves into thinking that simply recycling and composting, switching to compact fluorescent light bulbs, and buying hybrid cars will get us out of the jam we're in. These are important, but they're only a start. Our blind and relentless commitment to continued growth is the very heart of the crisis. If political leaders are serious about the economy being the highest priority, they'd better start to address the state of the global ecosphere. Climate change is the place to start.

Nature imposes the real bottom line

CANADIAN SPECIALTY TV channel Business News Network (BNN) interviewed me about the climate summit in Copenhagen in December 2009. My six-minute interview followed a five-minute live report from Copenhagen about poor countries demanding more money to address climate change and rich countries pleading a lack of resources. Before and after those spots were reports on the Dow Jones Industrial Average, the price of gold and the dollar, and the implications of some new phone technology.

For me, this brought into sharp focus the inevitable failure of our negotiating efforts on climate change. BNN, like the New York–based Bloomberg TV, is a twenty-four-hour-a-day network focused completely on business. These networks indicate that the economy is our top priority.

And at Copenhagen, money dominated the discussions and the outcome.

But where is the twenty-four-hour network dealing with the biosphere? As biological creatures, we depend on clean air, clean water, clean soil, clean energy, and biodiversity for our well-being and survival. Surely protecting those fundamental needs should be our top priority and should dominate our thinking and the way we live. After all, we are animals, and our biological dependence on the biosphere for our most basic needs should be obvious.

The economy is a human construct, not a force of nature like entropy, gravity, or the speed of light. It makes no sense to elevate the economy above the things that keep us alive. This economic system is built on exploiting raw materials from the biosphere and dumping the waste back into the biosphere. And conventional economics dismisses all the "services" that nature performs to keep the planet habitable for animals like us as "externalities." As long as economic considerations trump all other factors in our decision making, we will never work our way out of the problems we've created.

We often describe the triple bottom line—society, economy, and environment—as three intersecting circles of equal size. This is nonsense. The reality is that the largest circle should represent the biosphere. There are thirty million species, including us, that depend on it. Within the biosphere circle should be a much smaller circle, which is human society, and within that should be an even smaller circle, the economy. Neither of the inner circles should grow large enough to intersect with the bigger ones, but that's what's happening now as human society and the economy hit their limits.

We also draw lines around property, cities, provinces and states, and countries. We take these so seriously that we are willing to fight and die to protect those borders. But nature pays no attention to human boundaries. Air, water, soil that blows across continents and oceans, migrating fish, birds and mammals, and windblown seeds cannot be managed within human strictures, yet all the discussions in Copenhagen were centred on countries that, in turn, were divided into rich and poor. In science fiction movies where an alien from outer space attacks and kills humans, national differences disappear as we join forces to fight a common enemy. That is what we have to tap into to meet the climate crisis.

Nature is our home. Nature provides our most fundamental needs. Nature dictates limits. If we are striving for a truly sustainable future, we have to subordinate our activities to the limits that come from nature. We know how much carbon dioxide can be reabsorbed by all the green things in the oceans and on land, and we know we are exceeding those limits. That's why carbon is building up in the atmosphere. So our goal is clear. All of humanity must find a way to keep emissions below the limits imposed by the biosphere.

The only equitable course is to determine the acceptable level of emissions on a global per capita basis. Those who fall below the line should be compensated for their small carbon footprint while those who are far above should be assessed accordingly. And the economy must be aligned with the limits imposed by the biosphere, not above them.

6

It's Getting Hot Down Here

CLIMATE CHANGE IS a reality. We'd all love it if it weren't, if the deniers and industry PR folks were right. But mountains of scientific evidence and direct observation show that by burning fossil fuels, humans have added too much carbon dioxide to the atmosphere, which has contributed significantly to global warming. Other scientists and I have been warning about this for decades, and had we started to address the problem from the beginning, we'd be in a much better place today. But just as they did with evidence about the harms of smoking tobacco and the dangers of putting chlorofluorocarbons (CFCs) into the atmosphere, industry leaders and their paid PR people deny that there is a problem or that we could do anything about it if there were. The difference now is that climate change is a far more serious threat than smoking tobacco or putting CFCs into the atmosphere. Here we look at the science of climate change, the possible solutions, and the attempts by industry to delay or prevent action by sowing confusion.

Science is clear about
the threat of climate change

WHY DOES THE public often pay more attention to climate-change deniers than climate scientists? Why do denial arguments that have been thoroughly debunked still show up regularly in the media?

Some researchers from New York's Fordham University may have found some answers. David Budescu and his colleagues asked 223 volunteers to read sentences from reports by the Intergovernmental Panel on Climate Change (IPCC). The responses revealed some fundamental misunderstandings about how science works.

Science is a process. Scientists gather and compare evidence, then construct hypotheses that "make sense" of the data and suggest further tests of the hypothesis. Other scientists try to find flaws in the hypothesis with their own data or experiments. Eventually, a body of knowledge builds, and scientists become more and more certain of their theories. But there's always a chance that a theory will be challenged. And so the scientists speak about degrees of certainty. This has led to some confusion among the public about the scientific consensus on climate change.

What Budescu and his colleagues found was that subjects interpreted statements such as "It is very likely that hot extremes, heat waves, and heavy precipitation events will continue to become more frequent" to mean that scientists were far from certain. In fact, the term *very likely* means more than 90 per cent certain, but almost half the subjects thought it meant less than 66 per cent certain, and three-quarters thought it meant less than 90 per cent.

According to a February 2009 article in *New Scientist*, "Scientists Losing War of Words over Climate Change," the researchers concluded that scientists should use both words and numbers to express certainty. For example, the IPCC considers "virtually certain" to mean more than 99 per cent likely, "very likely" to mean more than 90 per cent certain, "likely" to be more than 66 per cent, "more likely than not" more than 50 per cent, and so on. It's important to understand the distinctions. People who recognize the urgency of the situation are more likely to get behind solutions. And businesses and governments are more likely to work toward solutions when the public demands that they do.

How urgent is the situation? The IPCC has concluded it is "very likely" that human emissions of greenhouse gases rather than natural variations are warming the planet's surface. Remember, that means they are more than 90 per cent certain. That's about as close to unequivocal as science gets. The IPCC has also concluded that the consequences could be catastrophic. This is science that has been rigorously peer reviewed and that has been agreed upon by the majority of the world's climate scientists, as well as more than fifty scientific academies and societies, including those of all of the G8 nations. There has been no credible peer-reviewed scientific study that has called into question the basic conclusions of the IPCC, which represents the consensus of the international scientific community.

So why does the debate still continue? Why are we fiddling while the world burns? Well, as Budescu's research shows, some people don't understand how science works. And people with vested interests, many of whom work with the oil and coal industries, are all too willing to exploit that lack of understanding by sowing confusion.

It's also true that many people fear change. We've seen examples of economic prosperity and job creation brought about by investments in green energy in places such as

Germany and Sweden. And leading economists have warned that not doing anything to confront climate change will cost us far more in the long run than acting now. But many people still fear that any profound change will upset the economy or diminish their quality of life.

We must also consider the rational argument for taking action on climate change. Even in the highly unlikely event that all of the world's climate scientists have got it wrong, if we still move forward to clean up our act, we'll end up with a cleaner planet and more sustainable technologies and energy sources. But if the scientists are right and we decide to listen to the absurd arguments of the deniers, we're in trouble. It doesn't seem like much of a choice.

We may never reach 100 per cent certainty about climate change and its causes—that's not what science is about—but one thing is certain: if we don't get together to work on solutions now, we'll have a much tougher time dealing with the consequences later.

Investigation hits at scientist's research

IN THEIR DESPERATION to find even a tiny shred of peer-reviewed science to challenge the volumes of research from around the world about human-caused climate change, deniers have often held up Willie Soon's work. Soon, an astrophysicist at the Harvard-Smithsonian Centre for Astrophysics, is known for studies that purportedly show that the sun, and not CO_2 emissions from human activity, is the main factor in climate change and that climate change in the twentieth century wasn't that unusual to begin with. He has also argued that mercury emissions from burning coal are no big deal.

In 2011, in response to a Greenpeace investigation, Soon admitted that U.S. oil and coal companies, including Exxon Mobil, the American Petroleum Institute, Koch Industries, and the world's largest coal-burning utility, Southern Company, have contributed more than $1 million over the past decade to his research. According to Greenpeace, every grant Soon received from 2002 was from oil or coal interests, despite the fact that he once told a U.S. Senate hearing that he had not been hired by, been employed by, or received grants from any organization "that had taken advocacy positions with respect to the Kyoto protocol or the UN Framework Convention on Climate Change."

Soon has also been affiliated with a number of industry front groups, such as the coal-funded Greening Earth Society and Koch-Exxon-Scaife-funded groups, including the George C. Marshall Institute, the Science and Public Policy Institute, the Center for Science and Public Policy, the Heartland Institute, and Canada's Fraser Institute.

Correspondence uncovered by Greenpeace also found that Soon led a plan in 2003 to undermine the Intergovernmental Panel on Climate Change's Fourth Assessment Report years before it was released in 2007.

It's not news that the fossil-fuel industry has funded an ongoing campaign of doubt and misinformation about the effects of its products and about the dangers of climate change—people and organizations from science historian Naomi Oreskes (co-author of *Merchants of Doubt*) to Greenpeace have been exposing these efforts for years. From hiring trolls and front groups to post comments on websites, submit letters to editors, and write opinion columns, to sponsoring "scientific" research and holding conferences, it's all been well documented. (The same tactics have also been used by the tobacco industry.)

The latest revelation is an embarrassment for oil giant Exxon Mobil, though. The world's largest oil company had admitted that it funded these efforts but promised in 2008 it would stop giving money to groups that lobbied against the need to find clean-energy sources. It's also an embarrassment for those who, in the face of overwhelming scientific evidence, deny the existence of climate change—or admit that it's happening but say we can't and shouldn't do anything about it. Of course, they will continue to repeat the same discredited points about "Climategate" and medieval warm periods and CO_2 as plant food, and they'll continue to take the advice of climate-change denial PR people like Tom Harris to bombard the media with opinion articles, letters to editors, and comments under online articles.

Some people rightly point out that we should look at the science and not at who is paying for the research. So what about Soon's science? Well, let's consider one paper that Soon published with colleague Sallie Baliunas, which attempts to discredit the work of Michael Mann, director of the Earth System Science Center at Pennsylvania State University. Three editors of the publication that ran the study, *Climate Research*, resigned in protest, including incoming editor-in-chief Hans von Storch. He said, "The conclusions [were] not supported by the evidence presented in the paper." Greenpeace notes also that thirteen of the scientists cited in the paper published rebuttals stating that Soon and Baliunas had misinterpreted their work. Meanwhile, Mann's work has repeatedly been verified by other scientific research, and numerous investigations have vindicated him.

After all their digging, deniers have been able to find only a few minor errors in the volumes of peer-reviewed science about climate change, and they have had to rely on manufactured scandals and conspiracy theories to bolster their arguments. It takes only a bit of investigating to poke holes in the scant bits of research that have attempted to discredit real climate science. Let's stop wasting our time on deniers. It would be better spent trying to resolve the serious problems we have created.

Science delivers repeated blows to deniers

IT MUST BE difficult, if not downright embarrassing, to be a climate-change denier these days. The scientists they've attacked have been exonerated, and more and more denier "experts" are being exposed as shills for industry or just disingenuous clowns. I use the term *denier* deliberately. People who deny overwhelming scientific evidence without providing any compelling evidence of their own and who remain steadfast in their beliefs even as every argument they propose gets shot down do not demonstrate the intellectual rigour needed to be called skeptics. Meanwhile, evidence that our fossil-fuel addiction contributes to dangerous climate change and harms the environment in other ways mounts every day, with oil spills, pipeline leaks, and other events. Let's take a look at some of what we are now learning.

Six independent investigations have found that the unimaginatively named Climategate was anything but the scandal or "nail in the coffin of anthropogenic global warming" that deniers claimed. After the illegal theft and release of emails from scientists at the University of East Anglia Climatic Research Unit, some reports found that the scientists could have been more open about sharing data; however, their science was rigorous and sound. The University of East Anglia has since posted its research and data online, and all of the emails in question have also been posted.

As for criticisms of the UN Intergovernmental Panel on Climate Change's global assessment of climate change, a review found that despite "a very small number of near-trivial errors in about five hundred pages," the report contained "no errors that would undermine the main conclusions." Yet another independent study supported Pennsylvania State University climatologist Michael Mann. Deniers have been attacking Mann's research for years.

Another blow to the deniers' arsenal came when London's *Sunday Times* was forced in June 2010 to run an apology and retraction for an article it published in January questioning the findings of the IPCC report on rainfall changes in the Amazon. The *Times* admitted that it had misrepresented the views of climate researcher Simon Lewis and that, contrary to its article, the findings of the IPCC report were backed by peer-reviewed research.

As their arguments fall apart, deniers have stepped up their efforts, even going so far as to send hate mail and death threats to scientists who are working to ensure our survival in the face of our greatest danger. Of course, the deniers will ignore the evidence. Nothing would please us more than if they were right. Life really would be easier if fossil fuels like oil and coal did not cause environmental damage or pose risks to life on our small planet and if they would last forever. But this is the real world, with real scientific evidence pointing to the urgent need to make changes in the way we live and get energy.

We have many ways to confront the threat of catastrophic climate change, from individual efforts to conserve energy and pollute less to government initiatives to encourage research and development into clean-energy technology. It's time to listen to the people who continue to look at the facts in the face of baseless accusations, break-ins, and threats. We need to listen to those who are trying to do something about our predicament rather than wishing it away.

Where's the climate conspiracy?

PEOPLE WHO DENY the reality of human-caused global warming were wetting their pants over the hacked emails brouhaha at the University of East Anglia Climatic Research Unit. In their desperation, the deniers claimed the emails pointed to a global conspiracy by the world's scientists and government leaders to... Well, it's hard to say what they believed the conspiracy was about. A letter to a Vancouver newspaper on December 21, 2007, indicates the way many of them think. The writer claimed that people working to address global warming "are ideological zealots pursuing a quasi-religious socialist agenda to command and control western economies."

This statement would be funny if it didn't echo the thinking of so many people—even some in influential positions in government and industry—and if the situation weren't so critical.

Sadly for the deniers and for all of us, the emails didn't show that global warming is a grand hoax or conspiracy. They did nothing to diminish the decades of overwhelming scientific evidence that not only is the earth warming, largely because of emissions from burning fossil fuels, but that it's worse than we thought. In 2009, twenty-six scientists from Germany, France, Switzerland, Austria, Canada, the U.S., and Australia released a report showing that the impacts of global warming are occurring faster and are more widespread than other reports from the United Nations Intergovernmental Panel on Climate Change had projected.

The report, titled "The Copenhagen Diagnosis," summarized research from around the world, which showed that Arctic sea ice is melting faster than we thought, that both Greenland and Antarctica are losing more ice than predicted, and that sea levels are rising more quickly than anticipated. The scientists concluded that the earth could reach several "tipping points" if we keep pumping emissions into the atmosphere at the current rate.

The report also quashes the myth of "global cooling" that has been "promoted by lobby groups and picked up in some media." The report's authors conclude that "even the highly 'cherry-picked' eleven-year period starting with the warm 1998 and ending with the cold 2008 still shows a warming trend of 0.11°c per decade."

It's astounding that those who deny that climate change exists or that it is human caused, either out of self-interest or ignorance, are willing to see some grand conspiracy in a handful of stolen emails but are unwilling to see the undeniably clear evidence of the impacts of climate change already occurring around the world. As University of Victoria climate scientist Andrew Weaver noted when many world leaders abandoned the idea of reaching a binding climate agreement in Copenhagen in 2009, those leaders are essentially saying that they don't believe they owe anything to our children and grandchildren.

Many government leaders argue that the economy takes precedence over the environment. But it's incredibly short-sighted to think that a healthy economy can be maintained when the health of the planet is failing. And it's absurd for any country to pin its economic hopes on extracting limited supplies of dirty fossil fuels in a world that is increasingly switching to cleaner forms of energy.

Forests are a piece of the global warming puzzle

WE STILL HAVE much to learn about the earth's mechanisms when it comes to regulating greenhouse gas emissions and global warming. Forests—along with grasslands, soils, and other ecosystems—are an important part of the equation, and a February 2009 report published in the scientific journal *Nature,* "Tropical Forests Grab Carbon," sheds a bit more light on their role. We've known for a long time that forests are important carbon sinks. That is, they absorb carbon from the atmosphere, thus preventing it from contributing to global warming.

But the *Nature* study shows that tropical forests absorb more carbon than we realized. Researchers from a number of institutions, including universities in Africa, Europe, and North America, analyzed data from 79 intact forests in Africa from 1968 to 2007, along with similar data from 156 intact forests from 20 non-African countries. They concluded that tropical forests absorb about 4.8 billion tonnes of carbon a year, equivalent to about 18 per cent of the carbon dioxide added to the atmosphere each year by burning fossil fuels. The world's oceans are the other major carbon sink, absorbing about half the human-produced carbon that doesn't end up in the atmosphere.

That doesn't mean we can count on the forests or the oceans to save us from our folly. To start, about 15 billion of the 32 billion tonnes of carbon dioxide that humans produce is not reabsorbed on land or sea and ends up in the atmosphere. And the carbon stored in forests can be released back into the atmosphere by natural disturbances, such as fire or insect outbreaks, or if the forest is logged. This is because when trees are cut down, die and decay naturally, or burn, some of the stored carbon is released back into the atmosphere. Even if carbon remains stored in the form of wood products taken from a logged forest, some is still released when soils in the forest floor are disturbed by logging. And many wood and pulp and paper products are discarded and destroyed in a much shorter time period than the life of an old-growth forest. This means that the carbon is released earlier than it would have been if the forests were left intact.

We humans have upset the balance of nature in more ways than we understand. The scientists haven't figured out why the tropical trees are growing big enough to absorb more carbon than they release. One theory is that global warming and the extra carbon in the atmosphere are actually fertilizing the trees. One thing we do know is that we cannot rely on tropical forests to prevent dangerous levels of climate change. But the amount of carbon they store gives us another compelling argument for protecting forests, as they may at least provide a buffer while we work on other solutions, such as reducing our energy consumption and switching to renewable sources of energy.

Clearly, this is not the only reason to protect forests. Looking at the ability of forests to absorb carbon allows us to see that they have economic value beyond resources that we have traditionally considered, such as lumber. Forests are a source of medicine, food, and clean drinking water and are habitat for more than half of all land-based plants and animals on the planet. Forests also provide spiritual, aesthetic, and recreational opportunities for millions of people.

Forest degradation is also contributing to another ecological crisis, a biodiversity crisis on par with earlier mass extinctions. Scientists estimate that sixteen thousand animal species are now threatened with extinction. Habitat destruction is partly responsible for this crisis, and climate change is exacerbating it. And although most of our carbon emissions are from burning fossil fuels, one quarter is from deforestation.

What all of this shows is that everything in nature is interconnected, and our planet works to find equilibrium. We can't confront the problems we have created on a piecemeal basis. We must look at them together. Conserving the world's forests—which can include sustainable forestry practices—is one obvious place to start dealing with global warming.

Protecting forests has many benefits

IN 1992, I attended an event that filled me with hope. Canada and the rest of the world had just signed a climate-change treaty at the United Nations Earth Summit in Rio de Janeiro. I remember being optimistic that the world could come together to fight the greatest threat to our planet and our own survival. We had done it before in overcoming other threats, like defeating Nazism in Europe and beating back horrific diseases like polio that once maimed and killed tens of thousands of people each year.

Climate change is now affecting people and places all over the planet, from the most remote tropical rainforest to the urban parks where many of our kids play. And scientists tell us that some changes, like melting sea ice in the Arctic, are happening much faster than any computer model had predicted. Although the 1992 United Nations Framework Convention on Climate Change (UNFCCC) treaty set no mandatory limits on greenhouse gas emissions and contained no enforcement provisions, it did set an ambitious science-based goal: to stabilize greenhouse gases in the atmosphere at a level that will prevent the effects of dangerous climate change.

Scientists say we can achieve this goal only if we radically reduce all major sources of heat-trapping greenhouse gas emissions. Although much of the debate and action has focused on curbing emissions from burning fossil fuels such as oil, coal, and gas, the destruction of our forests, wetlands, grasslands, and peatlands is responsible for about one quarter of all other emissions into the atmosphere. That's higher than emissions from cars, trucks, boats, and planes together.

Throughout the world, forests are being rapidly cleared for agriculture and oil and gas development and are being destructively mined and logged. When forest soils are disturbed and trees are burned or cut down for wood and paper products, much of the carbon stored in their biomass is released back into the atmosphere as heat-trapping carbon dioxide, though some carbon can remain stored in longer-lived forest products, like wood used to make furniture or homes. Thus the destruction of forests and other ecosystems is not only a driver of extinction of species, such as boreal caribou, but also a driver of global warming. We need to adopt a carbon stewardship approach to how we use our forests and the goods and services we take from them.

For some scientists, carbon stewardship means setting aside at least half of all remaining intact forests as protected areas, particularly carbon-rich forests like old-growth temperate rainforests in the north of Canada, Russia, Europe, and Alaska where wildlife like caribou feed, breed, and roam. Protecting intact forests also promotes ecological resiliency so that species and ecosystems can cope with and adapt to the effects of climate change.

That doesn't mean that the logging companies should be allowed to trash the other 50 per cent. Forests that we do manage for wood and paper production should be logged according to the highest standards of ecosystem-based management, without clear-cutting, and with adequate protection for wildlife habitat and sensitive areas like wetlands.

Scientists tell us that to avoid dangerous climate change, governments must agree to deep reductions in greenhouse gases, including carbon emissions from the destruction of our forests, wetlands, and other ecosystems. We can achieve this by agreeing to protect our intact forests, taking full responsibility for emissions from logging and other land-use activities, and helping developing nations reduce deforestation.

Let's use our forests in a truly sustainable way that is better for nature, better for the climate, and ultimately better for our own health and well-being.

Tree huggers versus smokestack pluggers

IF WE WANT to put the brakes on global warming and reduce our reliance on non-renewable fossil fuels, we must look to renewable energy such as solar, wind, hydro, and sustainable bioenergy. Given what the world's leading climate-change scientists are saying about the consequences of continuing to burn fossil fuels, we have little time to lose.

But the rush to develop new sources of clean energy has created surprising division among groups that should be allies in the fight against global warming: "tree huggers," who focus on the need to protect wildlife and wilderness, and "smokestack pluggers," who advocate for a rapid and massive increase in renewable-power production. In British Columbia, a coalition of environmentalists, resource nationalists, and public-sector unions called for a moratorium on new renewable-power production, citing concerns about impacts on biodiversity and the absence of proper government regulation, among other issues.

In response, Andrew Weaver, a Victoria scientist and lead author for the Nobel Prize–winning Intergovernmental Panel on Climate Change, argued in a March 2009 *Vancouver Sun* article, "Environmentalists Are Abandoning Science," that "some environmental groups have chosen to abandon science and campaign against clean energy and climate policies." Weaver went on to argue that "we need staggering amounts of energy conservation, emissions cuts, and renewable energy. And all need to be deployed at an unprecedented rate."

He's not alone in criticizing opponents of wind and run-of-river power. American environmentalist and writer Bill McKibben said in a March 2009 *Toronto Star* article, "The Fierce Urgency of Now," that "the environmental movement has reached an important point of division, between those who truly get global warming, and those who don't." He added, "When local efforts to delay or stop low-carbon energy projects come into conflict with the imperative to act urgently on global warming, they have to take second place."

I'm worried about the escalation of rhetoric on both sides. Yes, it is urgent that we find ways to tackle the problems caused by fossil-fuel use and excessive energy consumption. And it is true that some opponents of technologies such as wind power are motivated more by NIMBY self-interest than science or true environmental concerns. But that doesn't mean we shouldn't worry about the impacts of these projects and technologies. Nor does it mean that we should allow run-of-river power projects or windmills anywhere without proper government oversight and planning. Panic shouldn't guide policy.

It's ludicrous to think that we must sacrifice all environmental considerations to get green energy onto the grid. It's not green if it causes negative ecological impacts. In British Columbia, BC Hydro and the B.C. Transmission Corporation have identified more than 8,200 potential sites for run-of-river hydro projects in B.C.'s 291,000 watersheds. That should give us plenty of choice, and surely we don't have to harness all of them.

What we need, in B.C. and elsewhere, is to guide development toward areas that have high energy potential but are less susceptible to environmental damage. Governments must also act quickly to ensure that renewable-energy options are considered as a whole rather than in isolation. An individual project may appear to be environmentally benign, but the cumulative impact of many could be detrimental. We also need a better system for water licences and Crown land licences to avoid the gold-rush mentality that is leading numerous private interests to stake claims on rivers for power projects. And we need strong environmental regulations, along with monitoring and enforcement, to ensure impacts are minimized.

It's in our best interests to act quickly to get as much renewable energy into play as possible. As well as reducing our dependence on fossil fuels and combating global warming, renewable energy is one way to dig ourselves out of the economic mess we're facing. It's good for business. But that doesn't mean environmental safeguards should be relaxed in the name of green energy.

Global warming is, without a doubt, the most critical environmental issue we face. Clearly, there's no time to waste, but unless we tie our shoelaces before we race out the door, we're guaranteed to trip ourselves up long before we get to our destination. We need to ensure that our solutions don't lead to the destruction of the very thing we're trying to protect.

Technological fixes can have serious consequences

IN 1962, RACHEL CARSON galvanized a global environmental movement with her book *Silent Spring*. Before she wrote about the unexpected consequences of pesticides—including bioaccumulation of toxic molecules up the food chain—scientific innovations such as DDT dazzled us with their promise of greater control over the forces impinging on our lives.

We often look to technological fixes without acknowledging our ignorance about how the world works, and then we end up trying to correct the unexpected problems that result. When we began to use CFCs in large amounts, scientists had no idea they might affect the ozone layer. Salmon farms seemed like a good idea, but no one anticipated parasitic sea-lice outbreaks that would harm wild salmon.

Scientists find clever ways to tease out information about our world. And everywhere we look, we discover new challenges because our knowledge is so primitive. Accumulating pollutants in air, water, soil, and our bodies; vanishing species; loss of nutrients in topsoil; ocean degradation—all of these provide warnings that human numbers, consumption, and activity are undermining the very things that keep us alive.

Climatologists have accumulated a powerful set of observations and models pointing to fossil-fuel use as the cause of global warming. Obviously, the solution is to reduce the amount of greenhouse gases we create so that the biosphere can sop up the rest. Some imaginative suggestions would allow us to continue to burn fossil fuels without reduction: giant umbrellas in space to shield the earth from the sun, aerosols of sulphide to mimic volcanic emissions that reflect sunlight, and so on. Two that have attracted attention are iron seeding in oceans and carbon capture and sequestration on land.

The first involves putting iron into the oceans to fertilize waters where the lack of iron limits algae growth. In the lab, it has been shown that adding this iron to Antarctic Ocean water, for example, leads to massive increases in the algal populations. Companies have been formed on the promise that putting iron into oceans to induce algal blooms will help absorb carbon dioxide from the atmosphere. But in a 2010 paper in the prestigious journal *Proceedings of the National Academy of Sciences,* scientists reported that this process can cause the blooming of plants that produce deadly neurotoxins. Oops.

The second suggestion is carbon capture and sequestration. Canadian prime minister Stephen Harper has avoided discussion of the serious impacts of climate change on Canada and the economic implications of failing to reduce emissions. Instead, government policy is based on the fear that reducing emissions will be economically destructive, so we will wait instead for the development of methods to pump carbon dioxide into the ground. This technique is based on an observation that when carbon dioxide is pumped into depleted wells so that more oil can be recovered, the CO_2 doesn't come back out. This has led to a hope that we can capture much of the CO_2 from smokestacks, coal plants, and the tar sands and simply inject it into the ground—out of sight, out of mind.

But wait. Although we once thought that life petered out at bedrock, we now know that life exists up to three kilometres underground. Bacteria from deep underground are so different from anything we know above ground that we need entire new categories to describe them. Scientists estimate that the weight of all the organisms underground is greater than the weight of all life above it, including whales, trees, and people! Scientists know very little about the role these organisms play in the transfer of heat from magma or the flow of nutrients and water in the subterranean world, yet we are contemplating pumping millions of tonnes of CO_2 into that mysterious world.

We have so many ways to reduce our emissions and to save money and resources by becoming more efficient. Yet we avoid doing them on the hope of a totally untried technological promise that could have enormous negative consequences. Does this make sense?

Climate change and water flow together

NO ONE CAN live without water. In Canada, we like to think we're blessed with an abundance of clean water, but we really don't have a much larger sustainable supply of water than most places. We can sustainably use only the amount that runs off on land. What we do to the environment—and not just to the water itself—affects everything from the amount of water we have to the quality of our water supplies.

Climate change is already having a tremendous impact on water supplies, shrinking glaciers and causing more frequent droughts and flooding. A report by a Canadian Senate committee from 2005, "Water in the West: Under Pressure," put the issue in perspective: "Climate change means that precipitation is becoming less reliable, and more of it is expected to come as rain rather than as snow. What snow there is will melt sooner. There are likely to be more big storms and more severe droughts."

The report, which was based on expert testimony, also noted that summer flows in many Alberta rivers are down by about 40 per cent from where they were a century ago. It's not just a matter of less available water. As John Carey of Environment Canada noted in the report: "When we talk about climate variability we mean less rainfall overall in many areas, but the rain that does come will fall in intense events." Carey stated that "what we will face is too much water and too little water—too much in specific times and too little most of the time. We are saying that prairie droughts will be more persistent, and climate change may increase floods in duration and severity." We've seen a number of clear examples of this over the past few years.

Even the increased precipitation that occurs with climate change is not enough to make up for losses from melting glaciers and increased evaporation. Glaciers act like bank accounts, storing snow and ice during cool, wet weather and releasing water when we need it most, during hot, dry summers or years of drought. As University of Alberta ecology professor David Schindler wrote in an article titled "The Myth of Abundant Canadian Water," "Water scarcity will become one of the most important economic and environmental issues of the twenty-first century in the western prairie provinces."

As Schindler pointed out, though, "there is much that we can do to manage the problem." The solutions lie in both individual efforts and action from political leaders. To begin, leaders must deal with climate change. They need to commit to improving energy efficiency and implementing clean, renewable energy. They should discuss carbon-pricing strategies like cap and trade and carbon taxes. And they must figure out how to properly manage water resources and reduce water use.

On an individual level, people can conserve a lot of water—for example, by installing low-water-use plumbing and by landscaping yards so that they require less water—and governments can encourage water conservation through metering and creating disincentives for high water use.

A range of solutions from all levels of society is required, and those that address climate change—reducing greenhouse gas emissions, putting a price on carbon emissions, increasing clean-energy sources, for example—will create benefits beyond protecting our water supplies and reducing pollution. An economic analysis by the Western Climate Initiative showed that a plan to address climate change and foster clean-energy solutions among participating U.S. states and Canadian provinces could lead to cost savings of about US $100 billion by 2020.

We must all take the issue of climate change and its effect on water seriously. We can't live without water.

Ozone agreement shows possibility of progress

INTERNATIONAL LEADERSHIP based on sound science can lead to great results. For proof, we need only look up. The ozone layer is no longer shrinking.

Starting in the 1970s, scientists observed a connection between our use of chlorofluorocarbons, or CFCs, and a weakening of the ozone layer in the stratosphere. High above Earth, ultraviolet light breaks chlorine off the CFC molecule, and chlorine is a potent scavenger of ozone. Stratospheric ozone absorbs ultraviolet radiation, protecting us from the sun's rays like a giant pair of sunglasses. CFCs were once used in products ranging from aerosol spray cans to refrigerators. As more of the chemicals were dumped into the air, they began to destroy the ozone layer, creating the potential for dramatic increases in skin cancers and damage to the phytoplankton that form the base of life.

In September 1987, world leaders signed the Montreal Protocol on Substances That Deplete the Ozone Layer. In 2010, a report written and reviewed by three hundred scientists from around the world concluded that phasing out production and consumption of ozone-depleting substances under the Montreal Protocol "has protected the stratospheric ozone layer from much higher levels of depletion."

It's not a complete turnaround, but it is good news. The scientists found that global ozone and ozone in the Arctic and Antarctic regions are no longer decreasing, but they are not yet increasing either. They also wrote that "the ozone layer outside the Polar regions is projected to recover to its pre-1980 levels some time before the middle of this century." UN Environment Programme executive director

Achim Steiner noted that, without the agreement, atmospheric levels of ozone-depleting substances could have increased tenfold, causing "up to 20 million more cases of skin cancer and 130 million more cases of eye cataracts, not to speak of damage to human immune systems, wildlife, and agriculture."

Interestingly, the scientists and world leaders who worked to protect us from ozone depletion faced many of the same pressures that those working to protect us from climate change now encounter. CFC manufacturers claimed that the science on the dangers of CFCs was "rubbish" and that phasing out CFCs would cost trillions of dollars and would destroy the industry. As Naomi Oreskes and Erik Conway wrote in their excellent book *Merchants of Doubt*, many of the same "experts" show up in the campaigns industry has waged against the science regarding the impacts of tobacco, acid rain, and climate change.

If we can succeed in tackling the ozone problem, despite attacks from industry, why is it so difficult to resolve an even greater threat to life on the planet—climate change? One of the scientists who won a Nobel Prize for chemistry in 1995 for his work on the ozone layer has an explanation. F. Sherwood Rowland says that "arguing which propellant to use was rather trivial to society. One could replace CFCs and still use existing technology. This is quite different from having fossil fuels as our primary energy source for the whole world."

In other words, the stakes are higher—for industry and society. In many cases, CFCs could be replaced by something as simple and non-polluting as compressed air. And despite the claims of chemical manufacturers, phasing out CFCs did not bankrupt the industry, because these chemicals were only one product among many that the companies produced.

Although some energy companies are working on clean-energy technology, their massive profits come mainly from exploiting ever-dwindling supplies of fossil fuels. And pretty much everyone in the world relies on fossil fuels to some extent. The good news is that in the past two years, total worldwide investments in renewable electricity generation were greater than total investments in fossil fuel-based electrical capacity.

The solutions exist, but it will take a lot of effort and political will to make the shift. If we do it right, it will have enormous benefits for human health and economies. But don't expect the most profitable industry in the history of the universe to get on board any time soon.

It's up to all of us to demand change. The Montreal Protocol shows that progress is possible, but we must listen to reason rather than the claims of those who put profits before people.

We can't live without phytoplankton

EVIDENCE THAT THE world is warming, mainly because of our fossil-fuel addiction, and that this is having increasingly disastrous effects on our health and on the health of the planet's ecosystems, keeps growing. Meanwhile, arguments from deniers keep getting knocked down, to the point where one must conclude that there really are only two types of denier: those who are paid by industry to spread misinformation in attempts to confuse the public, which is criminal, and those who are unable to see the evidence staring them in the face and still cling to arguments that one minute with a good Internet search engine would dispel, which is pathetic and stupid.

One blow to the deniers came when the U.S. Environmental Protection Agency (EPA) examined in detail ten petitions challenging its 2009 finding that climate change is endangering the planet, that it is largely caused by burning fossil fuels, and that it threatens human health and the environment. In every case, the EPA found that the petitions misinterpreted data, contained false claims, and included exaggerated charges.

"The endangerment finding is based on years of science from the U.S. and around the world," said EPA administrator Lisa P. Jackson. "These petitions—based as they are on selectively edited, out-of-context data and a manufactured controversy—provide no evidence to undermine our determination. Excess greenhouse gases are a threat to our health and welfare."

Another report, published in 2010 by the U.S. National Oceanic and Atmospheric Administration, looked at data from 10 climate indicators measured by 300 scientists from 160 research groups in 48 countries. It concluded that human-caused climate change is undeniable and is increasing. So ice in the Arctic and in glaciers continues to melt, ocean temperatures and sea levels continue to rise, ecosystems and wildlife habitats continue to shift or degrade, and extreme weather events continue to become more frequent.

On top of that, a study by Dalhousie University oceanographer Boris Worm and his team found that phytoplankton populations in the ocean are declining at an alarming rate because of human activity and climate change. Why should we care? Well, these microscopic plants are the base of the food chain and account for half the production of organic matter on Earth. They also remove carbon dioxide from the air and produce more than half the oxygen we breathe. According to report co-author Marlon Lewis,

"Climate-driven phytoplankton declines are another important dimension of global change in the oceans, which are already stressed by the effects of fishing and pollution." The report, published in the July 29, 2010, edition of *Nature*, states that phytoplankton have declined by about 40 per cent since 1950.

We can't live without them.

While governments stall and deniers spread confusion, it gets more and more difficult to achieve the kind of emissions reductions that scientists say are necessary to prevent the earth from reaching a cataclysmic rise in global average temperatures. It was once possible, and may still be, but we are reaching a point where it will become impossible.

We all have a responsibility to do everything we can to reduce our own emissions, to vote for governments that make climate change a priority, and to make sure those governments focus on real solutions. We know that conserving energy and shifting to cleaner energy will not just help solve the climate crisis but will also resolve many pollution-related health issues and may even give economies a boost.

The fossil-fuel industry, which continues to reap multi-billion-dollar profits, has spent millions to support a handful of deniers, right-wing think tanks, and websites that call climate change "junk science" and deny human activity is influencing global warming. It's time we all started ignoring the insane blathering of the deniers. We've already wasted too much time on them—and we don't have time to waste.

7

Plumbing the Mysterious Depths

I **LIVE BY THE OCEAN**, and it's always held a special place in my heart. I also know how necessary it is to all life. More than half the oxygen we breathe comes from the oceans, and many of the world's people rely on protein from fish and other marine life. Many of our medicines come from the ocean. I've seen numerous changes in the oceans, locally and around the world, during my seventy-five-plus years. In British Columbia, salmon runs have been getting smaller every year, which in turn affects life in the oceans and along the rivers where they spend their lives, and in the forests that line the rivers and lakes. We've also heard about massive swirling patches of plastics and other wastes in the oceans. The truth is, we've been dumping garbage in our oceans and taking them for granted for too long. As you will see in this chapter, we can't live without healthy oceans.

. . .

International study is a wake-up call

IF WE CARE about ourselves and our children and grand-children, we must look beyond our immediate surroundings and do all we can to care for the oceans. But instead of respecting oceans as a life-giving miracle, we often use them as vast garbage dumps and as stores with shelves that never go empty.

The shelves *are* going empty, though. Humans are changing the chemistry and ecology of the ocean at a scale and rate not previously believed possible. According to a 2011 study from the International Programme on the State of the Ocean (IPSO), the combined effects of overfishing, fertilizer runoff, pollution, and ocean acidification from carbon dioxide emissions are putting much marine life at immediate risk of extinction.

The twenty-seven scientists from eighteen organizations in six countries who participated in the review of scientific research from around the world concluded that the looming extinctions are "unprecedented in human history" and have called for "urgent and unequivocal action to halt further declines in ocean health." The main factors are what they term the "deadly trio": climate change, ocean acidification, and lack of oxygen. Overfishing and pollution add to the problem.

The researchers also found that "existing scientific projections of how coral reefs will respond to global warming have been highly conservative and must now be modified." And they found that chemicals such as "brominated flame retardants, fluorinated compounds, pharmaceuticals and synthetic musks used in detergents and personal care products"—which can cause cancer and disrupt human endocrine and immune systems—have been found in aquatic animals everywhere, even in the Canadian Arctic. Marine litter and plastics are also found throughout the oceans, sometimes in massive swirling gyres.

Alex Rogers, the scientific director of the IPSO, is quoted in the *Guardian* as saying he was shocked by the findings: "This is a very serious situation demanding unequivocal action at every level. We are looking at consequences for humankind that will impact in our lifetime, and, worse, our children's and generations beyond that."

Action at every level means just that—actions that we can all take as individuals as well as actions that governments and industry must take. Reducing our own wastes, being careful about what we put down the drain, cutting down the amount of animal-based protein we eat and feed to our pets, and joining efforts to protect the oceans are a start, but the most important role we can all play is to tell governments and industry that we will no longer stand for this.

When reports like this come out, we often hear from industry-funded deniers and the dupes who help spread their misinformation, painting them as yet more conspiracies on the part of the world's scientists. And the response from governments is often to put industrial interests ahead of everything else. We must put a stop to this nonsense. Every year that we stall on the solutions to climate change means we are less likely to be able to resolve the problems. Other scientists and I have been warning about the consequences of climate change for more than twenty years, yet governments are still dithering while the world's natural systems continue to erode.

What this study also shows is that we cannot look at ecosystems, species, and environmental problems in isolation. This research points out that the combined impacts of all the stressors are far more severe than what scientists might conclude by looking at individual problems.

The report exemplifies the old adage about death by a thousand cuts. There is no single place to concentrate blame, except in the mirror. The study's authors note that "traditional economic and consumer values that formerly served society well, when coupled with current rates of population increase, are not sustainable." In other words, we need to account for the impact we have on the planet each time we flush a toilet, drink a pop, hop in a car, or eat a radish. There is no shortage of solutions, just a shortage of political will. Further delay in resolving these serious problems will only increase costs and lead to even greater losses of the natural benefits oceans give to us.

What we do to the oceans we do to ourselves

OUR PLANET, WITH its atmosphere, is an exquisitely interconnected system of ocean, air, and land. Water flows through all of it and keeps it—and us—alive. Water continually cycles above, on, and below the earth's surface, driven by the sun's energy. It evaporates from the seas, transpires from plants and soil, flows from glaciers and aquifers, and falls as rain or snow. It covers 71 per cent of the earth's surface. It can be liquid, gas, or solid. And it regulates the planet's temperature.

Part of the way water maintains a fairly steady surface temperature on Earth is by mixing with carbon dioxide to create a heat-trapping blanket in the atmosphere. But when we pump too much carbon dioxide and other pollutants into the air and water, it upsets the balance.

Even though our oceans and atmosphere are vital to all life, we often treat them as waste-disposal sites. We are putting more carbon dioxide into the atmosphere than the plants on land and in the oceans can reabsorb and process, so it builds up, trapping more heat and causing the planet's long-term temperature to rise. Many of the consequences of increased carbon dioxide have been widely reported, but global warming's effect on the oceans hasn't garnered the attention it deserves. As well as raising the temperature of the oceans, increased carbon dioxide concentrations cause acidification. The oceans absorb and store carbon, which makes them a good hedge against climate change. But when too much carbon ends up in the ocean, the ocean's pH levels fall and the water becomes more acidic.

Scientists warn that this could have a significant impact on coral reefs, perhaps even wiping them out entirely. If the reefs disappear, half of all life in the oceans will go with them. The process that affects corals—lower pH levels hindering their ability to calcify their skeletons—will also reduce the ability of phytoplankton to form calcium carbonate in their shells and skeletons. This, in turn, will reduce the ocean's ability to absorb and store carbon, leading to increased global warming.

Despite the warnings from scientists, ocean acidification hasn't been a big part of climate-change negotiations. We can't continue to ignore the state of our oceans. Of course, acidification—caused mainly by what we put into the air—is only one problem we've created for our oceans. We are also dumping a lot of crap (often literally) into our seas.

One of the most sickening images is of the giant plastic islands swirling in five ocean vortexes. One in the northern Pacific is estimated to be larger than Texas. According to the UN Environment Programme, thirteen thousand pieces of plastic are floating in each square kilometre of ocean, and much of it accumulates in the five large swirling ocean gyres. Marine animals eat the plastic as it breaks down, and contaminants work their way up the food chain, all the way to humans.

Scientists are looking for answers to this problem, and it's good to see that nations are now starting to come together in an attempt to address ocean acidification. But we must all do more to prevent these kinds of problems from occurring in the first place. We can do this by reducing our waste and emissions and by encouraging governments to show more leadership in protecting the earth and the oceans that cover most of its surface.

The oceans are where life is thought to have originated, as is indicated by the saltiness of our blood. The oceans flow through our veins and continue to give us life. Half of the oxygen we breathe comes from the oceans. What we do to the oceans we do to ourselves.

Blue Carbon report delves beneath the surface

TO MANY PEOPLE, our oceans are little more than a great blue expanse of water. To some, they are a source of beauty and enjoyment. And for millions of people around the globe, the oceans are sources of food and jobs in fishing or fish-farming industries. But the oceans are also the anchor for life on this planet. When it comes to global warming, the oceans may be our salvation.

The oceans do much more than provide us with food, employment, and enjoyment. They also absorb much of the excess carbon that humans have been pumping into the atmosphere during industrialization. The world's oceans have already absorbed a huge percentage of carbon that would contribute to global warming if it were released into the atmosphere, according to "Blue Carbon: The Role of Healthy Oceans in Binding Carbon," a report by the UN Environment Programme, the UN Food and Agriculture Organization, and the Intergovernmental Oceanographic Commission of UNESCO.

The IOC's Patricio Bernal argues that "the ocean has already spared us from dangerous climate change." He adds, though, that "each day we are essentially dumping 25 million tons of carbon into the ocean. As a consequence, the ocean is turning more acidic, posing a huge threat to organisms with calcareous structures." (These organisms include corals, clams, shrimp, and many types of plankton.)

The report finds that protecting and restoring marine ecosystems, such as estuaries and mangroves, could contribute to offsetting up to 7 per cent of current fossil-fuel emissions at a much lower cost than technologies developed to capture and store carbon at power stations. What this means from a global warming perspective is that by simply protecting and restoring these ecosystems, we could achieve 10 per cent of the reductions required to keep the climate from warming by 2°C. These actions would also have numerous other benefits to marine wildlife and fisheries.

The damage we are inflicting on ocean ecosystems has numerous consequences for global warming. Ice at the North and South Poles has kept ocean temperatures relatively stable for millennia. Now, the oceans are absorbing so much additional energy that the ice is melting and the oceans are warming at an ever-increasing rate. If polar ice disappears, the warming trend will escalate, because the albedo effect, the reflection of sunlight off bright surfaces like clouds and ice, will decrease. We can only guess how this will affect marine ecosystems and all life on our planet, but we are already noticing changes in the distribution and abundance of species throughout the world's oceans.

"Blue Carbon" notes that of all living organisms that are able to capture carbon, those that live in the ocean capture more than 55 per cent. Coastal wetlands, marshes, mangroves, and estuaries play an important role in absorbing carbon from the atmosphere. Other life forms in the open ocean assimilate carbon through their diets, which is then stored in the sediments of the deep ocean when the life forms die and sink to the bottom. This carbon will be stored for millennia.

Protecting more of these valuable ocean ecosystems will help control climate change resulting from excess carbon in the atmosphere and will also help restore the capacity of these areas to support marine life, particularly fish. Given that more than three billion people depend on marine fish for protein, we should do all we can to ensure abundant fisheries for the future.

The need for additional conservation of our oceans is undeniable, the benefits of doing so are becoming more evident every day, and the opportunity is before us. All we need now is for governments to acknowledge the leading science, like that presented in "Blue Carbon," and to get serious about investing in strategies that will put us on a more sustainable path.

We must find new ways to care for the seas

IT'S OFTEN SAID that we know as much about Mars and the moon as we do about our oceans. Considering that Earth is 71 per cent ocean, this should be cause for concern. At the very least, we should be doing more to protect our oceans from the negative effects of human activities, even if we don't fully understand all that is happening under the seas.

One thing we do know is that oceans are changing—and the changes aren't for the best. For centuries, we've thought of our oceans as stable. But ocean currents, upwellings, oxygen levels, acidity, and temperature are changing in ways we haven't seen before. Assumptions we once held about the seas are no longer valid. For example, we've always assumed that oceans would provide us with an endless bounty of food, but we are learning that is not true. The collapse of Canada's Atlantic cod stocks was just one of many warnings we should have heeded. Many west coast salmon stocks have also disappeared, and many are returning in increasingly lower numbers. Even the survival of the very base of the marine food chain, plankton, is being threatened.

Some threats to our oceans are easier to identify than others. Swirling garbage patches in the oceans are obvious artifacts of our disposable societies. "Dead zones" are showing up in our oceans around the globe. These are areas where oceans are starved of oxygen because of a nitrogen overdose from agricultural runoff. Many fish stocks are dwindling, in part because of our appetite for seafood. This is spurring more development in aquaculture—but most fish-farming practices are putting added pressure on oceans and wild fish.

On top of the many direct threats to ocean health, we also have climate change to contend with. We've seen that global warming is causing the oceans to become more acidic. This is a worrisome trend. As with our atmosphere, too much carbon is resulting in dangerous effects. Carbon dioxide is necessary for photosynthesis, which is how plants grow and develop. But when we burn fossil fuels or clear-cut forests, we release too much carbon dioxide into the atmosphere, upsetting the balance.

Science is confirming that our old assumptions are no longer valid, and we find ourselves in a situation of escalating risk. As a result, we need to look at our oceans in an entirely new way. We can't continue to exploit ocean resources on false assumptions. We need to know more about what's going on. That means investing in science that will help explain the interactions between changing ocean conditions and the species that depend on the seas.

We need a new way to manage our oceans in the face of uncertainty and elevated risk facing marine life. A comprehensive marine-planning initiative that considers new and evolving science and the evidence of what is actually happening to marine ecosystems would be a good start. This process must be based on a precautionary approach that recognizes increased uncertainty and the fact that our oceans will continue to change as global warming and other human-induced factors continue to affect them.

We can't rely on governments alone to protect the health of our oceans. Industry, non-governmental organizations, First Nations, coastal communities, and governments at all levels must come together to plan and monitor conservation efforts based on science and local community knowledge. After all, one thing we have learned about Mars and the moon is that we can't move there if we destroy our home on this beautiful and generous planet—in part because they don't have oceans. Neglecting the health of our oceans, where all known life began, is a risk we cannot afford to take.

Let's get it together with ecosystem management

THE NORTH COAST of B.C. is one of my favourite places. If you visit this spectacular and ecologically diverse region, you'll see people fishing, logging, travelling on boats and ships, and raising families. You'll see mountains, forests, oceans, sea lions, puffins, and whales. If you are fortunate to dive into the ocean, you'll see salmon, herring, rockfish, sea anemones, giant scallops, kelp forests, and—deep below—nine-thousand-year-old glass-sponge reefs. There is so much to see here, but we still have a lot to learn about how this ecosystem works.

It's absurd to think that we could manage our activities in such a vast and complex area by having different government departments oversee individual activities in isolation. But that's pretty much the way we've been doing things. Fortunately, people are talking about a new way of managing our oceans, a way that's being tested in five large ocean areas in Canada, as well as in New Zealand and the United States. One of these areas is the north coast of B.C., in a region stretching from northern Vancouver Island to the B.C.-Alaska border, which the Department of Fisheries and Oceans Canada (DFO) has labelled the Pacific North Coast Integrated Management Area, or PNCIMA.

DFO is attempting to engage an integrated management planning process here, in part based on the recognition that everything in nature is interconnected, including human activity. The concept was developed at the United Nations Earth Summit in Brazil in 1992 and is being considered in coastal areas in Europe, New Zealand, the U.S., and elsewhere. For years, many scientists, resource managers, and environmentalists have encouraged governments to adopt an ecosystem-based management, or EBM, approach that takes into account all values and interests. The electronic resource *Encyclopedia of Earth* defines EBM as "an integrated, science-based approach to the management of natural resources that aims to sustain the health, resilience, and diversity of ecosystems while allowing for sustainable use by humans of the goods and services they provide."

The federal government's planning processes in the Beaufort Sea, Gulf of St. Lawrence, eastern Scotian Shelf, Placentia Bay/Grand Banks, and Pacific north coast could set an example for the EBM approach in all of Canada's and many of the world's oceans. But until recently, there's been more talk than action.

The PNCIMA integrated management planning process has seen some significant breakthroughs, though. In December 2008, DFO signed a formal governance agreement with First Nations in the area to move forward with a marine planning process. And in March 2009, more than 380 people—including representatives from government, First Nations, coastal communities, marine industries, and non-governmental organizations—took part in a two-day forum to discuss management and conservation options for the region. That so many people from so many walks of life and so many communities were able to come together to discuss the needs of this area shows not just that cooperation is possible but also that everyone understands the need for urgent action to protect the health of our oceans.

As with most processes involving a multitude of resources, interests, and ecological values, the government must continue to play a leading role. Even more importantly, the government must provide enough money for scientific research to ensure that decisions are made according to the best local and scientific knowledge. Sadly, even though the government isn't putting in enough of its own money, in late 2011 it pulled out of a creative funding arrangement that would have injected the process with more than $8 million from conservation-minded philanthropic organizations.

We don't have a lot of time to waste. Many ocean ecosystems are at tipping points, with pollution, resource extraction, and industrial impacts contributing to declines in fish, mammal, and other marine-life populations. Add to that uncertainty about the effects climate change is having on these ecosystems, and the need for planning becomes even more urgent. A credible, long-term plan for any ocean region must include an increase in protected areas where specific types of industrial activity are limited. Canada has the longest coastline of any nation on Earth, and 40 per cent of our jurisdictional area is ocean, yet the federal government has set aside less than 1 per cent of that as marine protected areas.

I hope governments, First Nations, and other interested people will continue the formal dialogue, scientific research, and relationship-building required to ensure we have intelligent management and conservation of our oceans. I believe most people understand that our own health depends on the health of ocean ecosystems and are willing to come together to ensure that the ecological and economic well-being provided by our oceans are maintained at as high a level as possible.

Googling under water

THANKS TO AN initiative by Google, along with National Geographic, the BBC, and scientists and other partners from around the world, we're starting to learn more about what lies beneath the oceans. Google has added the world's oceans to its extensive Earth mapping. In a phone conversation with David Suzuki Foundation staff, John Hanke, director of Google Earth and Google Maps, admitted, "We had really overlooked two-thirds of the planet." Partly because of prodding from oceanographer Sylvia Earle, the company embarked on a massive project as part of Google Earth 5.0 to map the oceans using sonar imaging, high-resolution and 3-D photography, video, and a variety of other techniques and content.

Although the emerging picture is sometimes bleak, there's a positive side. "If we can just see enough soon enough to pull back and give these areas a chance to recover, that's my greatest hope," Earle told us.

Hanke and Earle, who is explorer-in-residence at National Geographic and the founder of the Deep Search Foundation, said the project will allow us to learn more about human impacts on the earth's oceans. Earle noted that we have explored only about 5 per cent of the ocean's depths and protected less than 1 per cent, yet the oceans cover more than 70 per cent of the earth's surface. The more we explore, the more fascinating things we find: strange and wonderful creatures, intricate corals, and ancient glass-sponge reefs.

"Some of these treasures are being destroyed before we even know what's there," Earle said, adding that often as soon as people find out about an ocean resource, they exploit it. Part of the idea behind Ocean in Google Earth is to show people what we have and what we stand to lose if we don't smarten up. "People will be aware of not only what's there but what's been lost," Earle said. "People don't seem to widely appreciate how important it is to protect the systems that give us life."

We can only hope this endeavour will lead to more concern for the state of the oceans and for the need to protect them. The glass-sponge reefs, for example, are being considered for formal protection, and public support could make the difference. As Earle noted, "You can't care if you don't know, and this a new way of knowing."

Part of what makes it exciting is that it's not just a tool for scientists and academics. "It's going to be a lot of fun for adults and kids to learn about the oceans," Hanke said, noting that the free program, which includes multiple layers of content and information, will continue to expand as more data from scientists, explorers, and others are added.

We can no longer afford to be blind to the state of our oceans. Let's hope this will open our eyes before there's nothing left to see but destruction.

Cruise ship industry needs better waste standards

IMAGINE WALKING DOWN the street just as the crew of an airplane flying overhead decides to dump sewage from the plane's toilets. Not a pleasant thought. Fortunately, airlines aren't allowed to do this. Cruise ships do it all the time, though—and not just with sewage, but with food waste, oily bilge water, and solid waste as well. As an article on the nonprofit news website DC Bureau, "Dirty Waters: Cashing In on Ocean Pollution," notes, cruise ship companies that rely on "pristine oceans, beautiful coral reefs, and marine life" and "that advertise excursions to untouched ocean scenery are threatening these very same natural resources with their standard practice of flushing harmful toxins, mostly as sewage and food waste, into the ocean."

Although some cruise ship companies have made improvements in waste-water treatment, the industry has a long way to go. And even though sewage is subject to some regulations, food-waste dumping is not regulated. Considering that a cruise ship can serve from 10,000 to 25,000 meals a day, that's a lot of leftover scraps and waste that are ground up and dumped into often-fragile ocean ecosystems. This waste becomes acidic as it decomposes, increasing nutrients that starve the ocean of oxygen and contribute to the creation of dead zones.

Cruise ship sewage can cause the same problems as food waste, and can also endanger the health of marine, bird, and human life by exposing them to fecal coliforms through direct contact or shellfish consumption. According to a report by Canadian researcher Ross Klein for Friends of the Earth U.S., titled "Getting a Grip on Cruise Ship Pollution," "A moderate-sized cruise ship on a one-week voyage with 2,200 passengers and 800 crew-members" can generate up to 210,000 gallons of human sewage, 1 million gallons of grey water (from sinks, baths, showers, laundry, and galleys), 8 tonnes of garbage, more than 130 gallons of hazardous waste, and 25,000 gallons of oily bilge water.

And that's just the stuff that gets dumped into the ocean. Cruise ships also generate a lot of air pollution from incinerators and the high-sulphur bunker fuel they generally use. The Friends of the Earth report notes that "on average, a cruise ship discharges three times more carbon emissions than aircraft, trains, and passenger ferries." Because cruise ships follow defined routes, this pollution is dumped over and over again in the same areas.

The technology to treat and properly dispose of the ocean waste isn't all that complicated, but it does cost money.

Marcie Keever of Friends of the Earth told DC Bureau that a good treatment system can cost between $1 million and $10 million. That may seem like a lot, but a cruise ship can cost more than a billion dollars to build. And because cruise ships, like a lot of ocean vessels, are often registered in countries with lax tax laws, their owners pay little tax on massive profits.

When it comes to regulating pollution from cruise ships, Canada has weaker laws than the U.S. and doesn't do a good job of enforcing the laws it does have. In the U.S., regulations vary from state to state. We need to strengthen laws, national and international, across the board, and we need to monitor and enforce those regulations to ensure that the industry is not harming ocean ecosystems.

Cruise ships offer a unique tourism experience and contribute to the economy, but none of this should be at the expense of the environment. Just because cruise ships are registered in countries with fewer regulations and tax laws doesn't mean the industry shouldn't have to follow the same standards as tourism businesses on land.

People who want to take a cruise ship vacation should check to see what kind of standards the ship and company have for environmental protection. (Friends of the Earth released an evaluation of the environmental and human health impacts of cruise ships and companies.) If the standards aren't good enough, customers should let the companies know that they will be willing to use their services only when they clean up their acts.

We should also consider telling federal politicians that we need marine-use plans, marine protected areas, and stronger regulations to limit the effects of increased cruise ship traffic on our most sensitive marine environments.

What the beluga can teach us

MANY PEOPLE WERE rightly outraged about news reports that coins thrown into a whale pool may have contributed to the death of a baby beluga at the Vancouver Aquarium in 2010. Regardless of the cause of one-year-old Nala's death—or what one thinks of whales in captivity—it was heartening to see that so many people cared.

But it would be nice to see that much attention paid to the stuff we humans throw into the belugas' natural Arctic habitat. We're killing more than just one baby beluga with our irresponsible actions. Of the seven beluga populations in Canada, three are listed by the Committee on the Status of Endangered Wildlife in Canada (COSEWIC) as endangered, one as threatened, and one as being of special concern. The other two are not at risk. The Cook Inlet beluga off the coast of Alaska has also been listed by the U.S. as endangered, and belugas have been listed as "near threatened" internationally. Along with hunting, the whales are threatened by "habitat loss from shore development, build-up of toxic contaminants and disturbance by commercial shipping, ice breaking and whale watching activities." Oil exploration and drilling in the Arctic could increase the risk.

Belugas aren't the only ones people are harming with the way we treat our oceans. We're hurting ourselves and our children and grandchildren as much as we're hurting the fish, whales, corals, and other life in the seas. And just as we can refrain from tossing coins into an aquarium whale pool, we can stop throwing our garbage into the oceans, and we can curtail some of the other activities that put marine life and our own lives at risk.

Just consider the giant garbage patches swirling in the Pacific and other oceans. All that plastic and debris doesn't get there by itself. Some of it comes from nets and garbage dumped from ships, but much of it comes from things discarded on land that get washed or blown into the oceans. These plastics and toxins end up in the stomachs of many marine animals, causing great harm, including death. Some of the toxins can also work their way into humans, as we eat the fish and other sea creatures. In fact, all of us carry a mixture of human-manufactured contaminants that have entered our bodies through the food we eat, the water we drink, the air we breathe, and the products and elements we come in contact with every day.

We also pour millions and millions of litres of oil into the ocean, through such disasters as the 2010 Gulf of Mexico oil spill. This illustrates how everything is interconnected—even our problems. The disaster in the Gulf was a direct consequence of our overconsumption and reliance on diminishing fossil fuels for energy. And that creates problems beyond pollution in the ocean. Our use of fossil fuels is also causing air pollution and is contributing to the greatest threat facing humanity: climate change.

What this should teach us is that all of us can and must do our part to turn it around. We need to drive less, consume less, use fewer plastic products, throw away less, recycle and compost more, and make sure the products we use are as environmentally sustainable as possible. These individual actions can make a powerful difference, especially because, as more people do their part, this becomes the socially "normal" way to live. Just look at some of the changes we've adopted in relatively short time periods: decreased rates of smoking where regulations and information have made the habit socially unacceptable, more people and stores shunning plastic grocery bags, more cities bringing in recycling and composting programs, more people cycling... The list goes on.

But it will take more than just making changes in our own lives. Action is needed in political and corporate realms as well. But remember that individual people wield the power in those institutions, and they must also respond to societal pressure. That's especially true of the politicians who are elected to represent the interests of all citizens. We must take democracy more seriously and be politically active to make environmental action a major part of the criteria in our voting choices. We need regulation and taxation to discourage what we don't want and to encourage what we want.

What we do in our lives affects our entire world—its soils, its rivers, lakes and oceans, its atmosphere, and all the living things that share our planet. We must understand that when we do something that harms the beluga or the grizzly or the spotted owl, we are also harming ourselves.

Basking in shame

THE BASKING SHARK is huge—often bigger than a bus. As fish go, it's second in size only to the whale shark. It has been roaming the world's oceans for at least thirty million years. Mariners throughout history have mistaken it for a mythical sea serpent or the legendary Cadborosaurus. Despite its massive size, it feeds mostly on tiny zooplankton.

These are some of the things we know about this gentle giant. But our understanding is limited; we don't really know much more about basking sharks than we did in the early 1800s. One thing we do know is that they used to be plentiful throughout the world's oceans. They were especially common in the waters off the coast of British Columbia, in Queen Charlotte Sound, Clayoquot Sound, Barkley Sound, and even in the Strait of Georgia. Only half a century ago, people taking a ferry from Vancouver to Vancouver Island may have spotted half a dozen lazily swimming by. But now, reported sightings are down to fewer than one a year off the B.C. coast. All indications show that this magnificent animal is on the edge of extinction. It makes my blood boil!

Over the past two centuries, people have been killing basking sharks for sport, for food, for the oil from their half-tonne livers, and to get them out of the way of commercial fishing operations. Many were also killed accidentally by fishing gear. Although they are now protected in many parts of the world, basking sharks are still popular in Asian markets, where their fins are used for soups and their livers and liver oil are used in medicinal and cosmetic products.

In their 2006 book *Basking Sharks: The Slaughter of B.C.'s Gentle Giants,* marine biologist (and David Suzuki Foundation sustainable fisheries analyst) Scott Wallace and maritime historian Brian Gisborne note that the "pest control" methods used in the 1950s and '60s were particularly gruesome. Basking sharks are so named because they appear to bask as they feed on plankton on the water's surface. And even though they don't eat salmon and other fish, they sometimes get tangled in gillnets, hindering commercial fishing operations. So fisheries patrol boats with large knives attached to their bows would slice the animals in half as they "basked" on the surface.

Basking sharks were not the only victims of fisheries-management practices during that time. Thousands of seals, sea lions, black bears, mergansers, and kingfishers were also killed in the name of reserving the salmon stocks for people. The Pacific basking shark was listed as endangered under the federal Species at Risk Act in 2010. It goes without saying that they need to be protected. The science is clear: the basking shark is Canada's most endangered marine fish. The Pacific population is almost extinct.

The decision to finally list the basking shark as endangered will have little or no economic impact, as there are so few sharks left. But recovery efforts are crucial, and because the federal government is largely responsible for the basking shark's demise, it must take responsibility for its recovery. Sadly, though, when it comes to vulnerable animals, science does not always seem to matter. For example, although the porbeagle shark is recognized as endangered by COSEWIC, Canada has failed to offer it legal protection under the SARA, and we still have a directed fishery for it.

Fisheries and Oceans Canada justifies this lack of protection for the porbeagle shark by claiming that the socio-economic impacts of listing it would be too great and that recovery and protection can be achieved by other means, such as the Fisheries Act. But as we can see from the example of the basking shark, those other means are not enough. Canada has been particularly bad in its treatment of the basking shark, but these animals need to be protected under strong species at risk legislation throughout the world. When one species goes extinct, the repercussions cascade throughout the environment. We can't afford any more losses.

8

Table for
Seven Billion?

THE SHIFT FROM being hunter-gatherers to farmers marked probably the biggest leap in human evolution. At first, it was relatively simple: people grew and raised food, harvested it, and then ate it, sometimes trading surplus with nearby folks. But as human populations grew, the challenge became how to feed more and more people, many of whom did not work on farms themselves. More than half the world's human population now lives in cities and urban areas. People in cold northern areas can eat strawberries year-round, and genetic modification has produced crops that are resistant to disease and pests. But, as with so much of what goes on in our lives, we must deal with unintended consequences of these supposed advances. Whether we're looking at food from farms or from harvesting wild plants and animals, we must be careful that we don't create more problems than we solve. As you'll see in this chapter, some have argued that because industrial agriculture is based on the mistaken premise that nature is inadequate and needs to be replaced with human systems, we must continually devise new solutions to the problems it creates.

Are your vegetables green enough?

Give me spots on my apples, but leave me the birds and the bees, please! —Joni Mitchell

ANY PARENT KNOWS that it can be a challenge to get kids to eat vegetables and some fruits. We've learned all the tricks: smothering broccoli with cheese sauce, putting peanut butter and raisins on celery sticks and calling it "ants on a log," convincing kids that eating spinach will give them Popeye muscles. Some kids just don't like the taste of certain fruits and veggies, and some have issues with the way the food looks. Adults are usually less picky about taste but can be finicky about the appearance of fruits and veggies. We've become accustomed to blemish-free produce. But what's wrong with a few spots on our apples?

According to the executives at two of the world's largest agricultural companies, Monsanto and Dole, our kids may be right: there is something wrong with spots, as well as the shape, texture, and taste of some vegetables. Or, at least, that's what they'd like you to think. The two companies have come up with a five-year plan to produce new varieties of spinach, broccoli, cauliflower, and lettuce with improved nutrition, flavour, colour, texture, and aroma.

I've never really had a problem with the way these vegetables looked or felt or tasted. But we now live in a world where square, seedless watermelons are seen as desirable and where companies like Monsanto can hold patents on genetically engineered seeds to grow food that has a uniform quality. The patents have allowed the biotech giant to sue farmers for "patent infringement" if the plants are found growing on their farms without a licence—even if the plants may have arrived by wind rather than design.

Monsanto was also one of the first companies to start commercially marketing DDT and has been a major producer of Agent Orange, Roundup, and other toxic chemical pesticides, as well as bovine growth hormone to increase milk production in cows. Dole has been involved in some controversies about its pesticide use, among other things, as well.

The issue isn't just about the agri-giants and pesticides and genetically modified foods, though. (In fact, Monsanto and Dole say their collaborative project to produce new vegetable varieties will be done through breeding and not genetic engineering.) The issue is about our relationship with food. Along with trying to maximize profits, the agriculture industry has made it possible for food to be transported around the world and for produce to keep longer without spoiling. These measures can benefit areas that have food shortages or short growing seasons.

They also mean, however, that we are giving up a lot of our control over one of the basics of life to large corporations that may not always have our best interests in mind. As Michael Pollan writes in his bestselling book *In Defense of Food*, eating goes beyond biological necessity: "Food is also about pleasure, about community, about family and spirituality, about our relationship to the natural world, and about expressing our identity."

Agribusiness will continue to play a role in our food production and delivery systems, but that doesn't mean we can't embrace some of the other trends emerging in the way we feed ourselves. As Pollan argues: "What we need now, it seems to me, is to create a broader, more ecological—and more cultural—view of food." That means eating more locally grown and organic food, eating less meat, steering away from processed foods, and not worrying about the odd spot on your apple. Or, as Pollan says in the opening of his book: "Eat food. Not too much. Mostly plants."

These small measures will help make us healthier, and they'll also make the planet healthier, by reducing the emissions generated in food production and transportation and by improving the ways we use our land base. Not only that, but they may even help get your kids to eat more vegetables. Carrots and peas are more fun to eat if your children grow and pick them from the garden. Come to think of it, we can all find spinach, broccoli, cauliflower, and lettuce with better nutrition, flavour, colour, texture, and aroma than some of the factory-farmed produce found on grocery-store shelves. We just have to look in the farmers' markets, or in our own backyard or community gardens.

With farming, bigger may not be better

WE OFTEN ASSUME the only way to feed the world's rapidly growing human population is with large-scale industrial agriculture. Many would argue that genetically altering food crops is also necessary to produce large enough quantities on smaller areas. But scientific research is challenging those assumptions. Taking a global approach to agriculture is critical. To begin, close to one billion people are malnourished and many more are finding it difficult to feed their families as food prices increase. But is large-scale industrial farming the answer?

Large industrial farms are energy intensive, using massive amounts of fossil fuels for machinery, processing, and transportation. Burning fossil fuels contributes to climate change, and the increasing price of oil is causing food prices to rise. Deforestation and ploughing also release tonnes of carbon dioxide into the atmosphere, contributing further to climate change. And industrial farms require more chemical inputs, such as pesticides and fertilizers.

Agriculture also affects the variety of plant and animal species in the world. According to a review of scientific literature by Michael Jahi Chappell and Liliana Lavalle, published in the journal *Agriculture and Human Values* in November 2009, agricultural development is a major factor in the rapid decline in global biodiversity. In their study, "Food Security and Biodiversity: Can We Have Both?," the authors note that agriculture, which takes up about 40 per cent of the world's land surface (excluding Antarctica), "represents perhaps the biggest challenge to biodiversity" because of the natural habitat that gets converted or destroyed and because of the environmental impacts of pesticide and fertilizer use and greenhouse gas generation from fossil-fuel use.

Large-scale agriculture also uses a lot of water, contributes to soil erosion and degradation, and causes oxygen-starved ocean "dead zones" as nitrogen-rich wastes wash into creeks and rivers and flow into the oceans. On top of that, despite the incredible expansion of industrial farming practices, the number of hungry people continues to grow.

Concerns about industrial agriculture as a solution to world hunger are not new. As author and organic farmer Eliot Coleman points out in an April 2011 article for Grist.org, "Organic Agriculture: Deeply Rooted in Science and Ecology," in the nineteenth century when farming was shifting from small scale to large, some agriculturists argued "that the thinking behind industrial agriculture was based upon the mistaken premise that nature is inadequate and needs to be replaced with human systems. They contended that by virtue of that mistake, industrial agriculture has to continually devise new crutches to solve the problems it creates (increasing the quantities of chemicals, developing stronger pesticides, fungicides, miticides, and nematicides, and employing soil sterilization, etc.)."

Volumes of research clearly show that small-scale farming, especially using organic methods, is much better in terms of environmental and biodiversity impact. But is it a practical way to feed seven billion people? Chappell and Lavalle point to research showing "that small farms using alternative agricultural techniques may be two to four times more energy efficient than large conventional farms." Perhaps most interesting is that they also found studies demonstrating "that small farms almost always produce higher output levels per unit area than larger farms." One of the studies they looked at, "Organic Agriculture and the Global Food Supply," concluded that "alternative methods could produce enough food on a global basis to sustain the current human population, and potentially an even larger population, without increasing the agricultural land base."

This is in part because the global food shortage is a myth. The fact that we live in a world where hunger and obesity are both epidemic shows that the problem is more one of equity and distribution than shortage. With globalized food markets and large-scale farming, those with the most money get the most food.

It's a crucial issue that requires more study, and the challenges of going up against a large industrial force are many, but it's hard to disagree with Chappell and Lavalle's conclusion: "If it is... possible for alternative agriculture to provide sufficient yields, maintain a higher level of biodiversity, and avoid pressure to expand the agricultural land base, it would indicate that the best solution to both food security and biodiversity problems would be widespread conversion to alternative practices."

We need to grow food in ways that make feeding people a bigger priority than generating profits for large agribusinesses.

Saving the berries for pickers and bears

ONE OF MY favourite summer activities is picking wild blueberries with my family at our cabin in northern British Columbia. The waning weeks of summer are the best time to be out in the bush, as the berries are ripe and flavourful, in contrast to the sometimes bland-tasting commercial varieties from the grocery store.

Wild-berry harvesting is a Canadian tradition that rural and northern people from Newfoundland to the Yukon share in late August. Wild blueberries have been an important part of the traditional diet of First Nations and Métis for generations, especially in the boreal forest, where several varieties, including the lowbush and velvet leaf blueberry, grow well in the acidic and nutrient-poor soils. According to University of Victoria ethnobotanist Nancy Turner, berry gathering has always been a social activity in Aboriginal communities. Family members and friends often set up berry-picking camps, where they will stay for days or even weeks to take advantage of nature's bounty. Berries are great fresh, but they're also tasty in jams, jellies, fruit leathers, and pies. They can also be sold commercially, which provides important seasonal income in rural and northern communities.

Our approach to managing the wild lands where these berries grow, such as the boreal forest, leaves something to be desired, though. According to prevailing economic thought, the only value in these areas is in the money we can make from harvesting or extracting resources—most often lucrative timber, oil and gas, or minerals. So when a natural forest is cleared, we replant it with a single tree species or a few economically desirable tree species of the same age and genetic stock, and then we try to maximize the growth of these species by using toxic chemicals to kill any insects or "competing" plants that would slow them down. These practices are common in many parts of the world.

It's time we started to recognize the significant economic importance of wild blueberries and other native plants—what rural economists call "non-timber forest products." For example, economists estimate that the Canadian boreal forest is worth between $261.4 million and $575.1 million a year to Aboriginal people for subsistence food alone. And these foods are increasingly becoming a delicacy for non-northerners. A pint of wild blueberries from northern Ontario sells for close to eight bucks in the trendy health-food stores of Toronto, where many consumers are motivated not only by the fantastic taste but also by increasing scientific evidence about the health benefits of the fruit.

Harvesting, processing, and selling wild blueberries brings pleasure and profit to many rural and northern communities. It's distressing that industrial activities, such as herbicide spraying by logging companies, can kill wild blueberry plants and other vegetation, which are considered competitors for resources needed by the trees, such as light, nutrients, and water. In Canada, the most popular herbicide for this purpose is Vision, produced by agrichemical giant Monsanto. David Suzuki Foundation science director Faisal Moola has studied the impacts of Vision herbicide on wild blueberry plants and has published research showing that chemical spraying harms the plants, reducing the number of berries available for people and wildlife like bears and birds. Logging companies typically spray the herbicide in mid- to late summer, which is when the berries are ripe. Because of this, wildlife and berry-pickers may also be accidentally exposed to chemical residues when they eat contaminated fruit (even though warnings must be posted when areas are sprayed).

Scientists continue to debate over whether Vision poses a serious risk to human and wildlife health. Still, some indigenous and local people have expressed concerns that chemical spraying could make the berries less healthy and are therefore reluctant to eat them. This indirect consequence of spraying herbicides in our managed forestlands is a concern. Wild berries are a free, healthy, and traditional source of nutrition for northern communities. If fears about toxicity, real or perceived, keep people from eating berries or the animals that graze on them, the consequences will be serious for people who are already ravaged by a Western diet of too much sugar, salt, and fat.

We should do everything we can to encourage people to eat safe and nutritious "traditional country foods," such as wild blueberries and other plants and resources of the forest (including wild fish and game). We must protect the traditional foods of First Nations and others who live off the land from the damage that industrial activities can cause.

More science needed on genetically modifying food crops

IN GEARING UP for the 2010 release of its super-genetically modified corn called SmartStax, agricultural biotechnology giant Monsanto used an advertising slogan that asked, "Wouldn't it be better?" But can we do better than nature, which has taken millennia to develop the plants we use for food? We don't really know. And that in itself is a problem. The corn, developed by Monsanto with Dow AgroSciences, "stacks" eight genetically engineered traits, six that allow it to ward off insects and two to make it resistant to weed-killing chemicals, many of which are also trademarked by Monsanto. It's the first time a genetically engineered (GE) product has been marketed with more than three traits.

Canada and the U.S. both approved the corn, and Canada has been criticized for doing so without assessing it for human health or environmental risk, claiming that the eight traits have already been cleared in other crop seeds—even though international food-safety guidelines that Canada helped develop state that stacked traits should be subject to a full safety assessment because they can lead to unintended consequences.

One problem is that we don't know the unintended consequences of genetically engineered or genetically modified (GM) foods. Scientists may share consensus about issues like human-caused global warming, but they don't have the same level of certainty about the effects of genetically modified organisms on environmental and human health! A review of the science conducted under the International Assessment of Agricultural Knowledge, Science and Technology for Development in 2008 concluded that "there are a limited number of properly designed and independently peer-reviewed studies on human health" and that this and other observations "create concern about the adequacy of testing methodologies for commercial GM plants."

Some have argued that we've been eating GM foods for years with few observable negative consequences, but as we've seen with things like trans fats, it often takes a while for us to recognize the health impacts. With GM foods, concerns have been raised about possible effects on stomach bacteria and resistance to antibiotics, as well as their role in allergic reactions. We also need to understand more about their impact on other plants and animals.

Of course, these aren't the only issues with GM crops. Allowing agrichemical companies to create GM seeds with few restrictions means these companies could soon have a monopoly over agricultural production. And by introducing SmartStax, we are giving agrichemical companies the green light not just to sell and expand the use of their "super crops" but also to sell and expand the use of the pesticides these crops are designed to resist. Continued reliance on these crops could also reduce the variety of foods available, as well as the nutritive value of the foods themselves. There's a reason nature produces a variety of any kind of plant species. It ensures that if disease or insects attack a plant, other plant varieties will survive and evolve in its place. This is called biodiversity.

Because we aren't certain about the effects of genetically modified organisms (GMOs), we must consider one of the guiding principles in science, the precautionary principle. Under this principle, if a policy or action could harm human health or the environment, we must not proceed until we know for sure what the impact will be. And it is up to those proposing the action or policy to prove that it is not harmful.

That's not to say that research into altering the genes in plants that we use for food should be banned or that GM foods might not someday be part of the solution to our food needs. We live in an age when our technologies allow us to "bypass" the many steps taken by nature over millennia to create food crops to now produce "super crops" that are meant to keep up with an ever-changing human-centred environment.

A rapidly growing human population and the deteriorating health of our planet because of climate change and a rising number of natural catastrophes, among other threats, are driving the way we target our efforts and funding in plant, agricultural, and food sciences, often resulting in new GM foods. But we need more thorough scientific study of the impacts of such crops on our environment and our health, through proper peer reviewing and unbiased processes. We must also demand that our governments become more transparent in their monitoring of new GM crops that will eventually find their ways into our bellies through the food chain.

Living la vida locavore

IN THE FALL, the bounty of farms, fields, and fisheries fills local markets. People around the world are embracing the idea of eating food produced closer to home, a sustainability movement that has been dubbed "locavorism." Proponents of eating local argue that we need to increase food security and reduce our dependence on other regions or nations for supplies of milk, meat, vegetables, fruit, cooking oil, grains, and other staples, as well as luxury items like fine wine and fancy cheese. According to the experts, the planet faces looming scarcities of almost everything necessary to sustain high crop yields—water, land, fertilizer, oil, and a stable climate. A disruption in global trade brought on by crop failure or skyrocketing oil prices could have serious consequences in many regions, especially in remote communities where much of the food must be imported.

The social and environmental benefits of eating local are also compelling. The globalization of food supply means that, on average, most of our food has to travel some 2,400 kilometres from field to table, resulting in enormous emissions of greenhouse gases and other atmospheric pollutants from the millions of trucks, container ships, trains, and other vehicles required to transport food around the planet.

For many people, the desire to eat local is motivated by the need for more information about how the food they eat is produced and prepared. Today, we are so disconnected from our food: processed and packaged foods, vacuum-sealed chicken breasts, garlic imported from China, apples from New Zealand, and the plethora of other cheap imported foods that have become little more than delivery systems for nutrients, calories, sugar, salt, and fat. If you buy your meat and fruit and vegetables at a local farmers' market, you can talk to the farmer or producer and find out what the chicken ate or how the potatoes were grown before you choose to put them on your dinner table. Many people would also argue that local food, because it is usually fresher, tastes better.

Although it is encouraging to see more people take greater responsibility for the food they eat by choosing to buy local, we can't let governments off the hook. Politicians need to support local agriculture by implementing policies and laws that protect farmland, ensure that farmers receive a fair price for the food they grow, and remove regulatory barriers that hinder farm-gate sales.

The protection of rich agricultural soil from urban sprawl, roads, industrial development, and other land use must be central to any government local food strategy. Study after study has shown that valuable agricultural land around the world is being chewed up and paved over because of poor urban-planning decisions that value parking lots, new highways, and larger strip malls over keeping our precious bank of fertile soil for current and future generations of farmers to steward—for our benefit.

A report by the David Suzuki Foundation, "Ontario's Wealth, Canada's Future," found that an alarming 16 per cent of farmland in the Greater Toronto Area was lost to urban encroachment between 1996 and 2001. This represents the loss of thousands of hectares of some of the most fertile soils in all of North America. The same is happening in other growing communities everywhere. We should all be concerned about these issues if we want to maintain local food security and minimize the environmental costs of the food we eat.

Shady practices make good coffee

COFFEE IS the second most traded commodity in the world, after oil. And as with oil, the massive scale of production necessary to meet our insatiable demand for coffee results in an enormous ecological footprint. According to the UN Food and Agriculture Organization, more than seven million tonnes of coffee will be produced worldwide this year.

The thirst for coffee is growing rapidly in developing countries, like Indonesia, where coffee beans are grown and exported. And while citizens of wealthier nations are cutting their coffee consumption, people in Africa and South America are drinking more—thanks to increasing household incomes, population growth, changing tastes, and successful marketing. The U.S.-based Starbucks Coffee Company has even expanded its operations to Africa.

With so many people drinking coffee, growers have industrialized production to meet demand. They've done this by establishing high-yield monoculture plantations, spraying toxic pesticides to control unwanted insects and plant pathogens, and even developing genetically modified varieties that allow traditionally shade-grown coffee, like arabica, to be grown under more economically productive conditions in partial or full sunlight. These industrial agricultural practices have proven successful in ensuring a steady supply of beans to world markets, but the environmental costs associated with much of the coffee consumed worldwide is too high, according to many scientists who study the industry and its impacts.

Much of the coffee sold in the U.S. and Canada is grown in open plantations on land that was once tropical or subtropical forest. Since the early 1970s, huge swaths of natural rainforest have been cleared in coffee-producing nations such as Mexico, as the industry has shifted from traditional shade production to "sun-grown." A sun-grown variety such as robusta can be planted at more than three times the density of arabica shade coffee. Because of this, most of the mass-produced and instant coffees you see on supermarket shelves are grown in this way.

Bridget Stutchbury, an internationally renowned bird expert who has studied the impacts of coffee production on neotropical birds, said in a lecture later reprinted and distributed by Birds & Beans Coffee that "sun coffee is not a self-sufficient ecosystem—it can only be grown with large amounts of fertilizer, fungicides, herbicides, and pesticides. There are no trees to shade the coffee plants and soil from the downpours of tropical rains; soil erosion and leaching is a big problem in sun coffee farms." On top of that, sun coffee plantations provide little habitat for sensitive species, such as neotropical migratory birds like the hooded warbler, which are threatened because of the loss of their rainforest habitat.

Troubled by the considerable environmental and social footprint of their favourite beverage, many consumers are looking for coffee that has been certified as organic, fair trade, or otherwise sustainably grown. But with so many choices, and confusing and difficult-to-verify environmental claims by businesses, experts recommend that you choose coffee that has been triple certified: organic, fair trade, and shade grown.

Although it won't replace natural forests, growing coffee in shade using agro-ecosystem techniques does provide extensive understorey and canopy cover from a diversity of tropical trees, providing a refuge for butterflies, birds, and other wildlife. Studies have shown that shade coffee plantations can provide habitat approaching natural conditions. For instance, a study in the El Triunfo Biosphere Reserve in southern Mexico found that the number of migratory bird species inhabiting a heavily shaded coffee plantation (thirty to thirty-five species) approached that of a natural rainforest (thirty-five to forty species). In contrast, sun coffee plantations were inhabited by fewer than five species.

As with food labelled organic or fair trade, consumers need a credible certification system to guarantee that their cup of coffee has been produced in a way that doesn't harm bird and other wildlife habitat. One credible certification system for shade coffee is the "Bird Friendly" eco-label, which is awarded to producers who follow a rigorous audit and verification process by the Smithsonian Migratory Bird Center. Switching to certified shade-grown coffee for your morning cup of joe won't save the planet on its own, but it is one more simple way to lessen your environmental impact.

Consumer demand spurs a corporate sea change

PROTECTING OUR PLANET is no longer seen as a fringe activity. Most people now consider themselves to be environmentally aware and are taking steps to help. Caring for the environment has become mainstream—it's the "new normal." And that's refreshing!

The environmental problems we face today are so serious that people from all sectors of society must work together to solve them. That's why it's so heartening to see an increasing number of corporations pitching in to protect nature and our planet's ecosystems. From restaurants to grocery stores to clothing retailers, businesses are looking for ways to make their operations more sustainable and environmentally responsible. They're taking tangible steps by offering better choices to consumers.

One of the best things about the growing number of environmentally responsible initiatives is that they demonstrate how powerful individual citizens can be. Businesses respond to consumer demand, and the right demands can result in real benefits for the environment. Some of the changes we've seen as a result of consumers using their power include reusable grocery bags, hybrid cars, locally grown and organic food in stores, products and clothing made with recycled materials, green buildings, and sustainable seafood in restaurants and stores.

So much can be achieved when people work together. Researchers at universities and environmental organizations often conduct studies and provide information. Citizens take that information and change their daily behaviour, sometimes by encouraging businesses to act on this new knowledge. Businesses respond by changing their practices and offering more sustainable choices. This in turn causes their suppliers to improve the way they produce their products.

One consumer trend that has been satisfying to me is the increasing demand for sustainable seafood. My grandparents came to Canada from Japan because of the abundance of fish in our oceans. My most cherished childhood memories are of camping and fishing in British Columbia. But over the years, I've seen a lot of changes. Many of the fish species that were once so abundant are now in decline, and some are facing extinction.

At the David Suzuki Foundation, we've worked hard over the years with our allied organizations in the SeaChoice program to scientifically assess which fish and seafood species are still thriving and which are threatened by overfishing and habitat loss. We've also looked at aquaculture practices to see which ones provide food without harming the environment and which have unacceptable impacts like spreading parasites and disease to wild fish. And we've been working with fisheries, aquaculture producers, and governments to translate the demand for sustainable seafood to real change in the oceans. After all, the end goal is to protect species and marine ecosystems. We've used this information to inform people about the best and worst choices for seafood. And individuals have responded by demanding that stores and restaurants offer sustainable choices and refrain from carrying species that are at risk or that are produced in a way that is harmful to the environment or to other species.

Fortunately, the tide has started to turn in Europe, the U.S., Canada, and other parts of the world. Many chefs, restaurants, and seafood distributors are working with SeaChoice and other sustainable seafood programs to offer better options. People everywhere should know that they can help businesses do the right thing by asking them to offer sustainable choices and by supporting businesses that do.

Fishing for salmon answers

MOST OF OUR FOOD, whether plant or animal, comes from farms. Notable exceptions are fish and other seafood, much of which is caught from wild ocean stocks. That's starting to change, though, as aquaculture plays an increasingly important role in the global food supply.

In many respects, that's good news, especially when wild fisheries are being harvested at or beyond a sustainable limit, and pollution and global warming, among other threats, are decimating wild fish stocks. When the aquaculture practices themselves start harming the wild fish, though, we must question whether or not the costs of farming outweigh the benefits.

Many aquaculture operations are environmentally sound, especially those that separate farmed fish from wild fish, such as the contained tanks and pond systems used to farm species such as tilapia and turbot. As well, many types of shellfish are farmed in ways that do not harm the environment. Yes, you heard me right: some types of aquaculture are okay. And yes, I eat some farmed seafood. But current salmon-farming practices are a different story. We've seen a lot of headlines about the damage done by salmon farms in many parts of the world. The scientific evidence is strong and growing, for example, that sea lice from salmon farms in British Columbia are causing severe damage to wild salmon stocks.

Sea lice are natural parasites that feed on salmon and are especially harmful to juvenile salmon, which don't yet have scales to protect them and which aren't normally exposed to sea lice in large concentrations. Sea lice multiply on salmon farms and attach themselves to juvenile salmon as they pass the farms on their way out to sea. Using drugs to control the lice isn't the answer, as the drugs come with their own environmental risks. At best, it is only a short-term solution, since sea lice are already developing resistance to the main drugs used to control them.

Research has demonstrated similar situations in other salmon-farming regions, like Scotland, Ireland, Norway, and Chile. In North America, a series of peer-reviewed scientific studies published in reputable journals, such as *Science* and the *Proceedings of the National Academy of Sciences,* has shown that sea lice can cause serious harm to wild salmon, including putting some stocks of pink and chum salmon at risk of extinction.

Wild salmon do not need additional threats to their survival. To put the issue in perspective, the west coast of Vancouver Island once boasted 1,200 stocks. Now, some 718—more than half—are extinct, at moderate risk of extinction, or considered stocks of special concern. At least 142 Pacific salmon populations have vanished forever.

Given the scientific evidence and the social, economic, and biological value of salmon, it is reasonable to expect change in the way things are done. Unfortunately, some people argue that the lack of 100 per cent proof means nothing should change. But scientific research rarely gives us such smoking guns. Nature is just too complex to even expect such a result. Science is a process of demonstrating the weight of evidence. Studies build on each other, eliminate alternative explanations, and test parallel ideas that help get to the most likely answer. In the process, other scientists have ways to challenge each other and test competing ideas. At a certain point, there is a solid reason to believe a given explanation is worthwhile. When something is as important as wild salmon, a strong weight of evidence justifies corrective action.

So what can we do? As a temporary solution, the salmon farms should be fallowed (removing the farmed fish for a period) while the juvenile fish pass by on their way out to sea. But the best solution would be to raise salmon in closed tanks that keep the farmed fish separate from the wild fish and their environments. Consumers should urge grocery stores and restaurants to sell only environmentally sound seafood products and should avoid buying products that are not.

Some people argue that it would cost too much to move to closed-system aquaculture or even to fallow farms during juvenile migration periods. But salmon shouldn't be seen just as a food source for people, and the costs of running any agricultural operation should include the money needed to ensure environmental safety as well as that required to build and run the farms. Wild salmon are a critical part of ocean, river, lake, and forest ecosystems. They provide food for everything from whales to eagles to bears and even help fertilize the forests along the shores, rivers, and lakes where they live and spawn.

Yes, everything is interconnected. If the wild salmon dwindle and die, next come whales, bears, and our forests. And where will that leave us?

Tiny sardines offer great guilt-free value

WHEN THE SIX-YEAR-OLD daughter of David Suzuki Foundation sustainable fisheries analyst Scott Wallace returned from a birthday party, excited about the hockey cards she got in her loot bag, her dad asked, "What players did you get?" She replied that she got the "sardine twins" from the Vancouver Canucks. Most hockey fans are aware of the value of the Sedin—not sardine—brothers to the Canucks, but we don't know much about the value of eating sardines and other small fish.

In 2010, renowned University of British Columbia fisheries scientist Daniel Pauly and his colleagues released a study in *National Geographic* magazine that looked at the global "seafoodprint," a measure of all the plant matter required to sustain seafood production. The higher up the food chain a seafood product is, the more photosynthetic energy is required to produce it and, therefore, the larger its seafoodprint. For example, eating a pound of tuna represents roughly one hundred times the seafoodprint of eating a pound of sardines, according to Pauly.

As long as harvests are tightly controlled to ensure that only a small portion of the total mass of living organisms is taken, eating species lower on the food chain takes much less of the world's ecosystem energy than eating higher up on the food chain and is therefore more sustainable. Species such as sardines, anchovies, herring, and mackerel—collectively categorized as small pelagic fish—already make up about 37 per cent of all fish landed from the ocean. The data are varied, but it appears that only about 10 to 25 per cent of small pelagic fish caught in the world are directly consumed by humans. The remaining 75 to 90 per cent are ground up into fish meal and oils to feed pigs, cattle, farmed salmon, and chicken, or are used as bait to catch larger fish—an inefficient use of perfectly edible protein.

Aside from their merits as a sustainable food source, small fish are inexpensive, typically caught without using a lot of fossil fuels, and are among the healthiest foods a person can eat. Health experts recommend that pregnant women eat sardines and similar seafood because they are valuable sources of omega-3 fatty acids, vitamins, calcium, and protein. Because these fish are found in tight schools, capturing them requires little chasing around, dragging of nets, or setting of lines, so their carbon footprint is low. Some research suggests that small pelagic fish may be the most efficient protein system in the world in terms of the energy used to capture them.

In 2009, sardine fishermen in British Columbia got about three cents a fish. I could go to Port Hardy during sardine season and buy a truckload for the price of an average Canucks ticket, $150. This same mass of halibut would cost about $15,000—one hundred times more. You'd think that any food that is tasty, healthy, sustainable, and cheap would be a preferred consumer choice, but direct per capita consumption of this type of fish in North America has dropped steadily since about 1985, and in 2008, the only remaining sardine and herring canning plant in the United States shut down. The trend in the U.K. and Europe is the opposite. There, small pelagic fish are steadily growing in popularity. In the U.K., demand for the Cornish sardine went from seven tonnes a year to eighteen hundred tonnes in less than fifteen years, an increase attributed to consumers wanting local, nutritious, and sustainable options.

Sardines are the second-largest fishery in Canada's Pacific waters. But about half of the British Columbia catch is sold as bait for the high-seas, long-line fishery for tuna—ironically, a highly unsustainable enterprise. Less than a fraction of a per cent is actually eaten by Canadians. On the Atlantic coast, only a small proportion of the herring caught is eaten by humans. The rest provide bait for the lobster fishery.

Sardines are a true rarity—a guilt-free food item. Every serving is one less used as bait or eaten by a pig, chicken, cow, or farmed salmon. Given the nutritional value of sardines and other small fish, it's possible that eating them is one of the secrets to the success of the Sedin brothers. After all, they're from Sweden, where small fish have always been a popular food choice.

What's the cure for the bluefin blues?

THE BLUEFIN TUNA is extremely valuable. One fish weighing about 340 kilograms sold for almost $400,000 in Tokyo's Tsukiji fish market in January 2011. But that's just the market value—which, sadly, appears to be the only value taken into account when we consider the bluefin or any other "resource."

The bluefin is economically valuable for a number of reasons. It's very tasty, prized by sushi lovers the world over, especially in Japan. Sport fishermen like it because it is powerful and fast and puts up a good fight. Unfortunately, the main reason the bluefin commands such high prices is that it has become precariously rare.

The bluefin tuna is unusual. Unlike most fish, it is warm-blooded, which allows it to migrate great distances, from the cold waters off Iceland to the warm waters of the Gulf of Mexico and the Mediterranean. Their unique colouring—steely blue on top and silvery white on the bottom—camouflages them from predators above and below. They can move at speeds of up to seventy kilometres an hour, thanks to their sleek shape and ability to retract their dorsal and pectoral fins. They have large appetites, satisfied by a varied diet consisting of smaller fish, crustaceans, eels, squid, and sometimes even kelp.

In the 1970s, increasing demand and prices led fishing companies to find more efficient ways to harvest bluefin. Stocks, especially of breeding-age fish, have since plummeted by more than 80 per cent over the past forty years. The bluefin is listed by the International Union for Conservation of Nature as "critically endangered." Although this has led to some conservation efforts, continued legal and illegal fishing of the bluefin is pushing the fish closer to the edge. In 2010, Japan led other nations to vote against a ban on fishing for bluefin at the United Nations' Convention on International Trade in Endangered Species.

And so, bluefin tuna continues to draw bidders at Tsukiji, the world's largest fish market. In the more than two decades since my first visit there, I've been amazed by the decrease in average size and in abundance of species such as bluefin and by the fact that seafood in Japan is brought to market from all over the planet.

In view of pronouncements by scientists about the imminent extinction of bluefin tuna and the possible emptying of oceans by mid-century, I asked some Japanese people to imagine their country without fish. "Fish are your history, your culture, your very physical makeup," I said.

But when I asked why Japan isn't then leading the fight to protect the world's oceans, I was met by blank stares—and this from people who are environmentally aware. Globalization has allowed the Japanese people to live on fish plundered from around the world, whereas only a century ago they lived on what their local waters contained.

One problem is the way we look at economics. There is no competing market for conservation of biodiversity—no one is willing to pay $400,000 to have fishermen leave this fish alone. Given the current demand—and prices—for bluefin tuna, it would be economically profitable to catch the very last fish. It would be worth someone's time to fish for four years just to land a single tuna. Meanwhile, other, less desirable fish stocks for which there are market substitutes tend to become unprofitable when the stocks get too low because the expense to catch them is greater than the market price.

Governments worldwide have contributed to the overexploitation of the bluefin and many other fish by subsidizing the commercial fishing industry with billions of dollars every year, much of it to build and modernize fishing vessels.

We must continue to call for a ban on fishing for bluefin and other endangered species and push for better regulation of and enforcement in global fisheries. As consumers, we should also increase our awareness about seafood and avoid eating fish that are in danger. It would also help if people in countries like Japan and China got serious about sustainable seafood. And it would be great if we could shift our thinking about economics to include the value of conservation and the services that ecosystems and plants and animals provide for us.

9

Healthy People, Healthy Planet

WE ARE INEXTRICABLY linked to the world in which we live. In some ways, the environment can be seen as an extension of ourselves. Every breath we take comes from outside, then is absorbed into our bodies to nourish us, and then is expelled once again. Water moves through us as well. The human body is about 60 per cent water. We take in food, extracting its energy and expelling the waste. Our own bodies provide ecosystems for trillions of living bacteria. It goes without saying that protecting our own health is an essential part of protecting the health of the planet. In this chapter, we look at how our health is affected by what we put on and in our bodies, and how our own health and the health of our environments are related. We also explore the latest findings in the nature versus nurture debate.

· · ·

Caring for ourselves, caring for the earth

ECOSYSTEMS COME IN all shapes and sizes, often without distinct boundaries. And what happens in one ecosystem affects other ecosystems. We can even consider the human body as an ecosystem, or perhaps more correctly as a number of interrelated ecosystems. According to a January 2010 feature in *Nature*, "2020 Visions," "The human body is one of the most important ecological study sites of the coming decade."

In his contribution to the feature, author David A. Relman, chief of infectious diseases at Veterans Affairs Palo Alto Health Care System in California, writes: "Humans depend on the microbial communities that colonize them for a surprising suite of benefits. These include: extracting energy from food, educating the immune system, and protection from pathogens. Yet, despite the recent attention to this indigenous microbiota, we are relatively ignorant of what our 'extended self' comprises or how it works."

If we didn't have microbes, which are mainly bacteria, living in and on us, we wouldn't be able to digest our food or breathe properly, and we'd be more vulnerable to numerous types of disease and infection. Scientists estimate that our bodies contain 10 times as many bacteria as human cells, numbering around 100 trillion, and that the human gut alone contains 500 to 1,000 species of bacteria. The microbes that help our body function properly are referred to as "normal flora" or "microbiota." But, like all ecosystems, our body's ecosystems can be disrupted. If we pollute our bodies, either intentionally or unintentionally, the normal flora can become overwhelmed to the point that they don't function as well as they should. Sometimes this may result simply in a case of upset stomach or indigestion, but often, especially if the pollution is ongoing, it can result in serious disease or death.

What we expose our bodies and the microbes within them to can also have unintended consequences. Although antibiotics have offered a lot of benefits to human health, we're now seeing that decades of their use, often as "growth promoters" in feed for chickens, hogs, and cows, is leading to new illnesses and infections as some bacteria evolve to be resistant to antibiotics and to our own microbial defences.

The more we learn about the microbial communities in our bodies, the more we see that a balance must be maintained, for our own sake and for the sake of our human communities. According to New York microbiology professor Martin J. Blaser, "Evolution has selected for those microbial populations that maintain and increase the fitness of both individual hosts and the group as a whole."

If we want our own bodies to be healthy, we must ensure that we have access to wholesome food, clean water, and good air. And we should avoid exposing ourselves to anything that would negatively affect the health of our own cells or the microbes that keep those cells healthy.

This is really no different than what happens in all ecosystems. If we put too much garbage and pollution into the air, water, or ground, we upset the balance created by all the organisms and natural cycles in the environment. Our planet itself has a lot of similarities to the human body. Water circulates around and through the earth in a complex hydrological cycle, regulating temperature and keeping plants and animals alive, just as blood circulates through our bodies. The natural organisms of the earth's ecosystems, like the microbes in our bodies, also offer numerous services that we rely on to survive and be healthy.

And for both the human body and the earth, carbon is an essential element. Carbon is the second-most abundant element in the human body, after oxygen, and it also cycles through the earth, its inhabitants, and its atmosphere. Normally, carbon is absorbed from the atmosphere through photosynthesis and is put back through respiration and decay. But when we upset the balance by cutting down too many of the plants or trees that absorb carbon and by burning fuels that put too much carbon back into the atmosphere, we put the earth's health, and thus the health of all of us, at risk.

We must learn to treat the earth as we would treat ourselves. After all, we are part of nature, and if we don't look after its health, we aren't looking after our own health.

What are you putting on your body?

EVERY DAY, WE slather ourselves with liquids, lotions, and potions—from shampoo and soap to deodorant and makeup. After all, most of us want to look and feel clean and to smell nice. It's not uncommon for a single person to use 10 or more personal-care products daily. We don't usually think of our cosmetics as a source of pollution, but U.S. researchers found that one eighth of the 82,000 ingredients used in personal-care products are industrial chemicals, including carcinogens, pesticides, reproductive toxins, plasticizers, and degreasers.

Take a look at the ingredient list on your bottle of shampoo or hand lotion. Most of us would have a hard time identifying which chemicals in the typically long list of ingredients may be harmful to human health or the environment. Chances are your personal-care products contain "fragrance" or "parfum"—often the last item on the ingredient list. Fragrance recipes are considered trade secrets, so manufacturers don't have to disclose the chemicals they include. More than three thousand chemicals are used to create "fragrances," usually in complex mixtures. Up to 80 per cent of these have never been tested to see whether they are toxic to humans.

These fragrances are found not just in perfumes and deodorants but in almost every type of personal-care product, as well as laundry detergents and cleaning products. Even products labelled "fragrance-free" or "unscented" can contain fragrance, usually with a masking agent to prevent the brain from perceiving odour. The negative effects of some fragrance ingredients can be immediately apparent, especially for the growing number of people with chemical sensitivities. For example, fragrance chemicals can trigger allergic reactions, asthma attacks, and migraines. Researchers have even found evidence suggesting that exposure to some of these chemicals can exacerbate or even contribute to the development of asthma in children.

Other chemicals may have harmful effects that don't show up right away. For example, diethyl phthalate (DEP) is a cheap and versatile chemical widely used in cosmetic fragrances to make the scent last longer. But it is associated with a range of problems. The European Commission report on endocrine disruptors has listed DEP as a Category 1 priority substance, based on evidence that it interferes with hormone function. Phthalates have been linked to early puberty in girls, reduced sperm count in men, and reproductive defects in the developing male fetus (when the mother is exposed during pregnancy).

Some research has also suggested that phthalate metabolites may contribute to obesity and insulin resistance in men. Health Canada has moved to ban six phthalates in children's toys after evidence showed that prolonged exposure can cause liver or kidney failure, but it has no plans to regulate the chemicals in cosmetics. DEP is also listed as a priority and toxic pollutant under the U.S. Clean Water Act, based on evidence that it can be toxic to wildlife and the environment.

Fragrance chemicals often harm the environment. Some compounds in synthetic "musk," which wash off our bodies and find their way into nature, remain in the environment for a long time and can build up in the fatty tissues of aquatic animals. Researchers have found measurable levels of synthetic musks in fish in the Great Lakes, and they've found that levels in sediment are increasing.

In response to the sensitivity many people have to airborne chemicals, a growing number of offices and public spaces are becoming "fragrance-free." This is a great initiative, but what are these and other harmful chemicals doing in our cosmetics in the first place?

The European Union restricts many fragrance ingredients and requires warning labels on products if they contain any of twenty-six allergens commonly used as cosmetic fragrances. Europe also prohibits or restricts the use of chemicals classified as carcinogens, mutagens, or reproductive toxins in personal-care products. It would benefit all of us to become more aware of what's in the products we use and switch to products that don't contain harmful ingredients.

Scents and sensibility

WE'VE ALL HAD the experience of a scent magically transporting us to a particular time or place. Some scents evoke meaningful memories, like frolicking in a field of flowers as a child or smelling the skin of someone near and dear. Some bring on different sensations, like a blinding headache.

Once, as I walked through a store's cosmetics department, the jumble of scents made me lightheaded and reminded me of an old maxim: your nose knows. Although the phrase entered the public's consciousness through a cartoon toucan shilling for a sugary breakfast cereal, it has some truth. Your sense of smell can often detect when things are amiss. When I walk into the store's potent cloud of perfumes, colognes, and fragranced body products, I get dizzy and I start to sneeze. My nose tells me that something isn't right.

In centuries past, the lack of basic sanitation and questionable personal bathing regimes might have made for some sticky, and stinky, encounters. So having some nice lavender oil or a spritz of floral essence to mask body odours would have been kindly appreciated by your kith and kin. Today, most scents don't come from local fields and gardens, but rather from far-off laboratories and overseas factories. And with running water and sanitation in our homes and workplaces, keeping personal odours under control shouldn't be much of a challenge. Yet, as a society, we continue to spend billions to bathe our bodies in artificial scents. The cosmetics industry has done a great job of casting a romantic light on its wares. These companies rarely miss an opportunity to present full-page ads and two-storey billboards with their products propped up by scantily clad supermodels to make synthetic scents seem sexy.

Although my disorienting trips through the cosmetics aisle are irritating to me, I know that for many people the aversion to chemicals used in personal-care products is much more serious. For some, exposure to these scents and fragrances can trigger acute health problems, ranging from disorientation to breathing difficulties and asthma attacks. What's more, some of the chemicals used as fragrance ingredients have been linked to chronic health issues like reproductive problems and cancer.

I'm happy that the office where I work had the foresight years ago to implement a fragrance-free policy. Groups like the Canadian Lung Association have long argued that workplaces should adopt policies to keep staff and guests from dousing themselves in scents before heading to the office. This is done as a courtesy to colleagues who are sensitive to such chemicals or who may simply not be as enthralled with the scent of the month, even if it bears the name of a hot celebrity or the hippest fashion label.

The one thing you won't find advertised on billboards, or even the ingredient list of your personal-care products, is exactly what chemicals are used in the fragrance mix. Manufacturers aren't required by law to disclose the ingredients used to scent, or sometimes "unscent," their products. Groups like the David Suzuki Foundation are demanding that the fragrance loophole be closed and that consumers be told what ingredients are in their products. Canadian author and broadcaster Gillian Deacon's book *There's Lead in Your Lipstick* and the American Campaign for Safe Cosmetics website are good resources for learning about toxins in cosmetic products and about products to avoid. Unfortunately, the list of things that fail the sniff test in our daily lives goes beyond the office and personal-care products. That new-car smell is really a host of harmful chemicals. Some air fresheners contain heavy metals. The smell associated with new vinyl shower curtains includes dozens of volatile chemicals that are bad for you. And of course, any kids' toys that smell like a chemical refinery when you open the packaging should be avoided.

These hazards are all too common, but using the sniff test is a good start. We can control the amount of fragranced products and chemicals that we bring into our home and work environment. Adopt fragrance-free policies. Shop wisely. Read ingredient lists. And use some common sense to avoid harmful scents.

Genome studies lead to unexpected results

SCIENCE OFTEN FOCUSES on a part of nature, isolating that part, then describing and probing it. This is called reductionism. Although the approach can provide powerful insights, it can also cause scientists to lose sight of the context or surroundings, which are intimately connected to the part being studied. A plant or animal in a flask or growth chamber is no longer subject to the light and temperature changes of day and night, the seasons, rain and wind, predation, or disease.

I spent almost four decades in one of the most reductionist of all sciences: genetics. This field of biology started gaining popularity in 1900, when the laws of heredity determining the behaviour of genes and chromosomes were discovered. The science hasn't been without controversy. It has been used to argue the "nature" side in the "nature versus nurture" debate, and it has led some to claim a genetic basis for everything from homosexuality, social class, and IQ to criminality, mental illness, and a range of diseases. With its focus on genetic causes for illness, the science has also to some extent absolved government, industry, and health professionals of their responsibility to limit possible environmental and social contributors to disease.

Still, it has been an exciting and promising field. With the acquisition of immense powers to extract, analyze, and synthesize genetic material, or DNA, scientists embarked on an awesome quest to determine the exact sequence of all three billion letters of the genetic code in a human genome. When I graduated with a PhD in genetics in 1961, I never dreamed that we would acquire such capabilities within my lifetime, yet by 2001, the Human Genome Project was complete. Billions of dollars were spent to map the human genome because scientists hoped to find the genes responsible for diseases like cancer, heart disease, and stroke. This knowledge, they thought, would allow them to design specific drugs and maybe even find a way to replace defective genes. For decades, we assumed that the Human Genome Project would reveal a hereditary basis for most diseases, just as they had been found for phenylketonuria, Huntington's chorea, Duchenne muscular dystrophy, sickle cell anemia, and cystic fibrosis.

The first surprise of the project was the relatively small number of genes found in humans. After all, we are complex animals, and researchers assumed our position at the top of the evolutionary ladder would be reflected in a greater number of genes than "lower" animals. Instead, scientists found that we have fewer than many other animal and plant species, and we share at least 95 per cent with our nearest relatives, chimpanzees. We now assume the number of genes isn't what distinguishes higher forms but the timing of gene actions and interactions.

Armed with the entire sequence of genes, scientists have also developed ways to compare genomes of groups carrying different diseases in the search for stretches of DNA that might be correlated with the conditions. This is referred to as genome-wide association, or GWA. According to Jonathan Latham and Allison Wilson of the Bioscience Resource Project, more than seven hundred studies examining more than eighty different diseases have all come up with similar results. Comparisons involving heart disease, cancer, stroke, autoimmune diseases, obesity, autism, Parkinson's disease, depression, schizophrenia, and other common illnesses reveal that many genes may have a tiny influence but none can be considered the major factor underlying the condition.

This is a stunning revelation that some geneticists find difficult to accept because it means designer drugs and genetic engineering to target or replace a genetic defect are not the answers. Billions of dollars have been and are being spent on GWAs and the search for major genetic determinants of disease. It's time to accept the reality that they won't be found and that we must instead turn to the challenge of addressing the more important contributors to human disease: malnutrition, lack of exercise, and polluted air, water, and soil.

And, as Latham and Wilson argue, "The laying to rest of genetic determinism for disease... raises the stakes by confronting policy-makers as never before with the fact that they have every opportunity, through promoting food labelling, taxing junk food, or funding unbiased research, to help their electorates make enormously positive lifestyle choices."

Let's not take abundant clean water for granted

IF YOU'RE READING this in Canada, the U.S., Europe, or Australia, chances are good that you can go to your kitchen and pour yourself a glass of cold, clean drinking water straight from the tap. If you've had a stressful day, you can run yourself a nice warm bath. That's not the case in some parts of the world, where a woman may have to walk many kilometres with her children just to fill a bucket with murky water, which she must then carry back over the parched landscape. Canadians and Americans who have travelled outside of the tourist resorts in nearby Mexico know that abundant and clean water is never taken for granted there.

In the U.S., climate change is expected to reduce flows in major rivers, including the Rio Grande and Colorado, by as much as 20 per cent this century, according to a report by the Department of the Interior. With an increase in droughts over the past several decades, river basins in the western U.S. and other areas are already experiencing challenges in supplying growing populations with water for drinking, irrigation, power generation, and recreation.

We often take our abundant and clean water for granted, but we shouldn't. To begin, climate change is altering precipitation patterns, increasing drought in some areas and flooding in others, and it's reducing the amount of water stored in glaciers, snow packs, lakes, wetlands, and groundwater. At the same time, demand for water and threats to clean supplies are increasing as our populations grow and as industry, especially in the energy sector, continues to require greater amounts. Despite technological improvements, the tar sands use considerable amounts of water and pollute rivers and groundwater. Hydraulic fracturing, or fracking, requires massive amounts of water to extract natural gas from shale deposits, and the process is known to contaminate water supplies. Nuclear power plants also require vast amounts of water.

The consequences of water shortages and contamination are severe and numerous. Many of us remember the tragedy in Walkerton, Ontario, in 2000, when 7 people died and as many as 2,300 became ill after drinking from wells containing high levels of E. coli bacteria. It's an issue that many First Nations in North America have to deal with every day. In fact, around the world, water-related illness is one of the leading causes of death, mainly in the developing world. Health authorities estimate that unclean water kills 3 million people a year, including close to 2 million children who die of diarrhea because of bad water. Worldwide, researchers estimate that as many as half of the people in hospital are there because of waterborne diseases.

Water shortages also mean less is available for irrigation, which has a severe impact on our ability to grow food. As University of Alberta ecology professor David Schindler has argued, "Water scarcity will become one of the most important economic and environmental issues of the twenty-first century in the western prairie provinces." A 2005 Canadian Senate report concluded that summer flows in many Alberta rivers are already down by about 40 per cent from where they were a century ago. We must also consider what will become of people as water becomes more scarce and contaminated. Along with the other issues around climate change, this could trigger massive refugee crises.

Fortunately, solutions exist. As individuals, we can conserve water. Canadians and Americans use twice as much water per capita as Europeans and many times more than people in most parts of the world. By raising awareness of our consumption, installing low-flow plumbing, and using landscaping that doesn't require much water, we can all make a difference.

Governments have a huge role to play as well. To start, metering and disincentives for high water use can help with conservation. But most importantly, governments must tackle the challenge of climate change. Along with protecting clean water supplies and human health, addressing climate change will strengthen the economy. An analysis conducted in 2010 by the Western Climate Initiative showed that addressing climate change and fostering clean-energy solutions could lead to cost savings of about US$100 billion by 2020 for the initiative's member states and provinces.

We can't live without clean water. That's something we all have to think about.

UN knows that forests are vital to health

THE UN GENERAL Assembly met in New York to declare 2011 the International Year of Forests. The idea was to raise awareness of the priceless role that forests play in keeping the planet healthy and of the need for sustainable management and conservation of all types of forests. The International Year of Forests follows other lofty proclamations by the UN to encourage efforts to advance social justice and environmental sustainability, including the 2010 International Year of Biodiversity, the 1993 International Year for the World's Indigenous People, and the somewhat unusual naming of 2008 as the International Year of the Potato.

It's easy to be cynical about the annual declarations made by our world leaders, especially as there's often a lack of corresponding action. Nevertheless, the International Year of Forests marks a critical moment on our planet. Our forest ecosystems have never been at more risk from the consequences of human actions, including climate change and industrial activities. But a few events, including the signing of the Canadian Boreal Forest Agreement, offered hope that 2011 would truly be the Year of Forests.

The world's remaining forests, from true wilderness like the boreal forests of Russia and Canada and the tropical forests of Latin America to urban green spaces like the forested slopes that frame Vancouver, represent a Fort Knox of natural riches. Forests remain our primary source of paper and building materials and are receiving increasing attention as a source of bioenergy—functions that sustain millions of jobs in resource-based communities around the world.

Forests provide food, clean drinking water, and life-saving medicines like the rainforest-sourced cancer drug vincristine. They are also home to millions of indigenous peoples and habitat for more than half of all known terrestrial biodiversity on the planet. And because they sequester and store billions of tonnes of carbon in their vegetation, peat, and soils, forests are a critical shield against runaway global warming. Canada's boreal forest alone stores an estimated 208 billion tonnes of carbon, the equivalent of twenty-six years worth of global greenhouse gas emissions from fossil-fuel burning.

Despite the importance of forests to biodiversity, as well as to our own health and well-being, we continue to destroy them at an alarming rate. Throughout the world, forests and woodlots are being ripped up and developed, degraded by free-for-all oil and gas development, and mined and logged at a blistering pace. Less than a fifth of the world's original intact forests remain, and although much of the best of what's left is found within Canada's borders, the country is falling down when it comes to looking after its national natural heritage. Canada continues to clear-cut wilderness habitat when alternative logging methods exist, it has no national strategy to ensure that remaining ancient temperate rainforests are protected, and provinces like B.C. continue to export millions of raw logs to be processed out of the country.

At the same time, no nation was better placed to deliver on the ambitious goals of the International Year of Forests than Canada. With the Canadian Boreal Forest Agreement, twenty-one forestry companies and nine environmental groups committed to present a joint vision to federal, provincial, and territorial governments and First Nations for protection and sustainable management of Canada's boreal. This included new protected areas, world-class forestry practices, and promotion of environmentally sustainable Canadian forest products in the marketplace.

The success of the Canadian Boreal Forest Agreement will depend on whether Aboriginal people and their governments are involved and their rights as decision-makers are respected. Where indigenous peoples have come together with environmental groups and other stakeholders, stunning victories have been achieved.

More than half of the ancient rainforests of Haida Gwaii on Canada's west coast have now been protected, thanks to the leadership of the Haida First Nation. In Central Canada, 5 Anishinaabeg First Nations communities in eastern Manitoba and northern Ontario are working to have a vast intact region of boreal forest declared a UNESCO World Heritage site. Covering no less than 43,000 square kilometres, the area is called Pimachiowin Aki in Ojibwa, which means "the land that gives life."

Forests sustain the very life-support systems of the planet—clean air, pure drinking water, productive soil, and healthy wildlife populations. It's time we recognized our interdependence with them and treated them as the biological treasures they are.

Driving home the benefits of staying active

I WAS STRUGGLING through my routine at the gym when the owner came up to me. "Give me something to share on Twitter for Earth Day," he demanded. I've been working out for more than thirty years and I'm still waiting for it to be fun, or at least easy, so my brain was not operating at full bore. I panted, "How about this? Get out and exercise. It's good for your body and it's good for the environment." He seemed happy enough and wandered away, but his question got me thinking.

I'm a biologist. I know that we evolved out of the natural world and lived without machines for a long time. Everything our ancient ancestors did, they did by expending some effort, especially to get from one place to another. Our bodies evolved to keep up with this required effort. Indeed, our bodies need to work in order to restore themselves. Don't believe me? Just look at one of the most effective ways to reduce the risk of heart disease, diabetes, Alzheimer's, stroke, cancer, and more: exercise!

Now, I know that a car is an amazing piece of technology, but it's just a means of getting us from point A to point B. When we climb into a car to drive five or ten blocks instead of walking or cycling, we may come up with all kinds of rationalizations as to why it was necessary, but do we ever stop to consider that this simple act works against what our bodies need? When I walk by a school and see roly-poly kids jumping from the big cars lined up outside, I suspect that parents think they're doing their children a favour. But it's at the expense of what kids need to remain healthy. If a neighbourhood is so dangerous that we can't let our children walk to school, then we should work to make it safer, or initiate group walks.

When a ninety-kilogram person climbs into a two-thousand-kilogram vehicle, more than 95 per cent of the gasoline is burned to move the car, not the person! That's a lose-lose-lose situation: we throw away money, waste energy, and exacerbate environmental pollution. The auto sector has dazzled us with big, fancy stuff because energy has been cheap and the environmental consequences haven't figured in its planning. With the near-death experience of the big three auto companies as the economy melted down, and with oil prices rising steadily, car companies are finding religion on being green as they tout smaller, more efficient cars. Let's hope this represents a turning point in the values that motivate them.

But we also need to shift the way we all think of cars. People seem to regard a car as an extension of themselves— bigger, sexier, noisier, faster, more powerful. I can understand the psychology, but still, it's just a machine. It's something to get us to our destination, but it has become so deeply embedded in our culture that it's impossible to think of doing without it—at least until we build cities in ways that eliminate our need for personal vehicles. Our love of cars also sets a bad example for the rest of the world, especially China and India, where growing economies are creating huge numbers of people with the means and the desire to buy vehicles.

These days, you can find all kinds of books offering ten or one hundred easy ways to save the planet. But the planet is not in trouble. Whatever we do, it will continue to spin and move around the sun. We may be in trouble, though. We're altering the chemical, physical, and biological features of the biosphere, making it increasingly difficult for tens of thousands of species, including our own, to survive and flourish.

Changing course and reining in our demanding appetite and economy is not going to be easy. If everyone buys an electric or hybrid car, changes light bulbs, and carries cloth bags, we'll still be a long way from a sustainable way of living. But thinking about our own personal health and our relationship with machines may at least get us started down a new road.

Our children spend less time outdoors than ever before in history. But how does sitting for so long in front of computers or TV screens affect our kids—not to mention the rest of us? To begin, people who lose their connection to nature and the outdoors can lose their desire to protect it. People also see themselves as being apart from nature and its wonders, rather than being intricately connected to the biological systems that keep us alive and healthy. For example, they may grow up into adults who design urban spaces that are cut off from the very life that sustains us. But there's also the truth that all of our parents knew: getting outside into the fresh air is good for your health—physical and mental. We adults have created a lot of the problems the world is now facing. It's time for us to set a better example for our kids by teaching them that they are a part of nature and they must respect it as they respect themselves.

· · ·

Outdoor fun is good for children and the planet

WHEN I WAS growing up in London, Ontario, in the early 1950s, back doors would flap open between 5:30 and 6 PM, and parents would call Johnnie or Mary to come home for dinner. We'd be out playing in the park, empty lot, or nearby ditch or creek. Back then, there wasn't a television station in London, and the few folks with TV sets had to capture signals from Cleveland or Detroit and watch shadowy black-and-white images made worse by electronic snow. There were no computers, cellphones, iPods, or digital anything. Our fun was outdoors.

Now, according to author Richard Louv, only 6 per cent of nine- to thirteen-year-old children in the U.S. play outside in a typical week. This is reflected by a dramatic decline in fishing, swimming, and even biking. Louv, co-founder of the Children & Nature Network, noted that in San Diego, "90 per cent of inner-city kids do not know how to swim" and "34 per cent have never been to the beach."

I live near the ocean in Vancouver, and when my children were in primary school, I would watch the tide charts for exceptionally low tides so that I could take my daughters' classes to the beach. It always surprised me to see how many of the kids had never been to a "wild" beach. Some were timorous about walking about in the muck of a tidal flat. Most had never turned over a rock to find crabs, blennies, and anemones. Often, the immediate reaction was "Yuk," but I never found a child who wasn't entranced within a few minutes to find these natural wonders. Now that I'm an old man, my sentiments may simply reflect nostalgia for the "good old days." Children today find it hard to fathom the world of my childhood. "What did you do?" they ask in amazement. They can't imagine a world without all of the electronic accoutrements of their instant, plugged-in world.

The eminent Harvard biologist E.O. Wilson coined the term *biophilia*, referring to our need to affiliate with other species (*bio* = life; *philia* = love). He believes this need is built into our genes, a reflection of our evolutionary roots. In cities, we increasingly work against our biophilic needs by instilling a biophobia. We teach our children by the way we react to nature's intrusion into our homes: "Take that out. Don't touch. It might bite." This is a problem, because the way we treat the world around us is a direct reflection of our values and beliefs. Compare the way we treat another species when we believe it is our biological kin rather than just a resource, commodity, or opportunity. The way we see the world shapes the way we treat it, and we will protect only what we know and love.

But our cities have developed with more regard to the needs of cars and commerce than people. When a father has to go to court to fight for the right of kids to play road hockey—as I read in a news article recently—you know something is wrong. Globalization has disconnected us from the real world as we purchase products for their brand names without regard for the source of the raw materials or where and under what conditions the components were manufactured and assembled. Food no longer reflects seasons or locale. It becomes easier to focus on the economy and consumption, while forgetting the real source of everything we need and use, namely, nature.

Our children have exchanged the experience of outdoors and nature for the enclosed world of electronics, resulting in "nature deficit disorder," as Richard Louv calls it. For those of us who are concerned about the state of the biosphere, this is disturbing, because a person for whom nature is a stranger will not notice, let alone care about, environmental degradation.

That's why many environmentalists are concerned about the way young people are growing up. Computers, television, video games, and the Internet offer information and entertainment in a virtual world without the hazards or discomfort of mosquitoes, rain and cold, steep climbs, or "dangerous" animals of the real world—and without all the joys that the real world has to offer. Unless we are willing to encourage our children to reconnect with and appreciate the natural world, we can't expect them to help protect and care for it.

Breaking down the school's walls

WHEN OUR CHILDREN and grandchildren head back to school every fall, it's important to consider not just what we're teaching them but how we're teaching them. After all, the world is facing some incredible challenges, and today's young people will be left to deal with many of them. So, do we fill their heads with facts and figures so that we can evaluate their progress through standardized testing? Or do we give them tools so that they can think for themselves?

In 1956, when I was in college, Rachel Carson, a biologist, writer, and ecologist who had a tremendous influence on me, wrote an essay for *Woman's Home Companion* magazine, titled "Help Your Child to Wonder," which she later expanded into her book *The Sense of Wonder.* In the article, she wrote, "It is more important to pave the way for the child to want to know than to put him on a diet of facts he is not ready to assimilate."

Carson believed, as I do, that we humans are just one part of nature but that our ability to alter natural systems is what sets us apart. And we often alter natural systems in detrimental ways because we do not understand or appreciate nature. Carson argued that instilling in young people a sense of wonder about the earth and its marvels and mysteries will make them care more about nature and the environment. And she also thought that it would help them lead fuller lives. "Those who dwell, as scientists or laymen, among the beauties and mysteries of the earth are never alone or weary of life," she wrote in the article.

More fulfilled people in a healthier world—it sounds ideal. But how do we accomplish that? Carson described the value of just getting kids into nature to explore. Doing so will even make the inevitable—and useful—facts and figures that will follow more relevant. "If facts are the seeds that later produce knowledge and wisdom, then the emotions and the impressions of the senses are the fertile soil in which the seeds must grow," she wrote. But in this age of computer games and text messaging, of standardized testing and declining education budgets, kids are spending less time outdoors than ever before. Parents have a responsibility to get their children outside, but our schools and teachers must play a role as well.

How can we expect our children to become fulfilled and healthy if we neglect to teach them or inspire them to become interested in their place in the natural world? Sure, we can include the natural sciences in curricula and teach them from books and computers alongside reading, writing, and arithmetic—but most children learn and retain information better through direct experience. Scientific studies have also shown that humans have an innate affinity with nature and that spending time in nature has immense psychological benefits.

In fact, moving the learning environment outdoors as much as possible will not only give young people an appreciation for nature and the planet that sustains us, but it will also help with other learning. Studies have shown that spending time in natural environments helps with recall and memory, problem solving, and creativity. Children (and adults) who spend more time outside are also physically healthier.

The possibilities are endless. Think of how much more interesting and valuable math would be if it were made less abstract by relating it to natural phenomena, such as calculating the height of a tree. Reading the work of someone like Rachel Carson makes you realize how inspiring nature can be for any kind of writing, from poetry to scientific analysis. It goes without saying that subjects such as biology and geography would be more relevant if taught outdoors. That doesn't mean all schooling should be moved outside, but we must try at least to increase the amount of time learning takes place in nature.

Instilling a sense of wonder and joy about nature at an early age ensures that biophilia (a love of and affinity with nature) rather than biophobia (a fear of or discomfort with nature) becomes the predominant trait as people grow. Given the deteriorating state of our natural world, this is a compelling reason for moving the classroom outside.

Teach your children to be well

MY GRANDSON'S NICKNAME is Gunny. What a joy it is to escape the complexities of adulthood to focus on him, just playing. One day when he was eighteen months old, I had to muck out the compost on a typical Vancouver winter day—it was pouring rain. So I dressed Gunny up in boots, sweater, gloves, and rain slicker, and out we went.

As each shovelful turned up worms, I encouraged Gunny to pick out the big ones to feed to the turtle. He dove in with gusto. Anything moving and colourful immediately attracted his attention. It took a while to empty the fully composted side of the box and turn over the newer material, but he kept digging away with his toy shovel and never lost interest or wandered off.

I cannot imagine what is going on in my grandson's brain. He is learning about an entire world with no reference points to start from. A while back, his other grandfather was chopping wood, and, as he was piling up the pieces, there was Gunny, barely able to walk, struggling to carry a piece of wood to the pile! Composting? Piling wood? One might wonder what meaning those activities will have for a child who is going to grow up in a big city, parked in front of a computer screen or text messaging on a cellphone. I believe they have everything to do with that child's future. You see, I am as alarmed by the astonishing rise of childhood obesity as I am about the ecological crisis. Children learn by the example set by adults.

When my daughter Severn was twelve years old, she gave a speech at the Earth Summit in Rio de Janeiro in 1992, appealing to adults to think more about children and the kind of world we are leaving them. Her words struck a nerve and created a media flurry. At one point, a reporter commented, "Yeah, we've done a pretty lousy job of taking care of the environment, but you kids are different; you'll lead the way." It was an attempt to compliment her, I suppose, but I was astonished by her reply. "Oh," she said, "Is that the excuse for adults to do nothing? Besides, you are our role models. We copy what you do, so how can you expect us to be any different?" I was dumbstruck by the depth of her response. She was absolutely right. How many parents who smoke are successful when they tell their children not to smoke? "Do as I say, not as I do" is a pretty weak way of trying to influence a child's behaviour.

That brings me back to my grandson's generation. If they are surrounded by role models who are too busy to spend time playing, who watch television or play computer games to pass time together, how are they going to know that walking, jumping, and moving are what our bodies need to stay healthy? We evolved from the natural world where everything we did involved our muscle power. Harnessing the power of animals was a huge advance, but on an evolutionary scale, it was extremely recent. Our bodies must move to stay healthy.

Exercise is an important factor in reducing a number of our major health problems, from diabetes to stroke, Alzheimer's, heart disease, and cancer. Our bodies evolved to be active. But since we started harnessing cheap, plentiful energy in oil, we've used machines to do our every bidding. Exercise, like concern for the environment, shouldn't be a special activity for which we need experts, gyms, and equipment. It has to be a part of the way we live.

Moving, walking—anything involving the expenditure of energy—is exercise. Driving a few blocks instead of walking or biking, or using escalators and elevators instead of stairs deprives our bodies of what they need to stay healthy. Even though I prefer to get my exercise from everyday activity, I go to the gym—but not to look buff. (At my age, that is a long-gone hope.) I do it for my health. Exercise is my medicine. Now that energy prices are rising, we have a chance to rethink the way we live. We must include exercise as an important health component. In the meantime, as a caring grandfather, I want to spend more time hiking and playing with my grandchildren.

We shouldn't expect kids to clean up our mess

I TURNED SEVENTY-FIVE in March 2011. That means I probably won't be around to see the worst impacts of climate change or any other looming environmental disasters—or the much brighter future that may emerge if we get off our butts to address the problems. But I'm also a father and grandfather, and because I care about my children and grandchildren, and all of the world's children, I continue to work and to speak out about environmental challenges and solutions.

Climate change is already having noticeable impacts around the world, including food shortages, increasing extreme weather events, shrinking glaciers and ice caps, and rising sea levels. We've already upset the atmospheric carbon balance, so the more we ignore the problem, the worse it will get. It's unconscionable that we would condemn our children and grandchildren to an increasingly bleak future, especially when readily available solutions would help to resolve many other global problems. Cleaner sources of energy would reduce pollution and the health problems that go along with it. Improving social justice would help give people the time, resources, and inclination to focus on considering environmental issues and improving their quality of life. Reducing our reliance on fossil fuels would resolve crises that threaten political and economic stability.

It shouldn't be up to young people to clean up the messes we have made. After all, we don't even allow them to vote—to choose who will make decisions on their behalf. And they will be most affected by the decisions made today. But because so many adults have abdicated their responsibility to the world and its children, youth are taking matters into their own hands.

One young person in the U.S., Alec Loorz, even took his government to court over its inaction on climate change when he was just sixteen. He and others launched actions against state and federal governments in an attempt to have the atmosphere declared a "public trust" that must be protected, a concept that has been used to clean up polluted rivers and coastlines. "We will let the world know that climate change is not about money, it's not about power, it's not about convenience," he said. "It's about our future. It's about the survival of this and every generation to come."

Alec Loorz started an organization called iMatter when he was just thirteen. He has rallied youth from around the world to march during the second week of May every year to raise awareness about climate change. He argues that children have "the moral authority" to ask their parents and leaders, "Do I matter to you?" It's a question that deserves an answer. For many adults, the honest answer would have to be, "No, we're more concerned about cheap gas, the economy, profits for the fossil-fuel industry, and having more stuff."

Reading about Alec Loorz reminded me of my daughter Severn's speech at the Earth Summit. She asked the delegates, "Are we even on your list of priorities?" She also reminded them that "losing a future is not like losing an election or a few points on the stock market."

Severn is now a mother herself, and I'm proud that she takes her commitment to her child and to all children seriously. As well as being a great mom, she works hard to raise awareness about environmental issues through her writing, speaking, and TV appearances. We owe it to our children and grandchildren to help clean up the messes we've made. We also owe them respect and support when they get involved and push us to do more for the world. Parents must become eco-warriors on behalf of their children, because their future should be as important to us as it is to them.

10

Life, the Universe, and Everything

WHAT DOES IT TAKE to be an environmentalist? What lessons can we learn from our relatively short history on Earth? What does evolution teach us? I've long pondered some of these questions and thought about the lessons my parents have taught me, the knowledge I've gained from the people I've met and worked with, and the things I've learned from reading everything from fables to scientific reports. When I look at my own life, and the history of humans and their relation to the planet, I see that change really is the only constant. Despite numerous setbacks, we've always found ways to survive and prosper. Looking at the big picture gives me hope that we can still find ways to live well on this amazing small blue world.

. . .

Is seven billion people too many?

WHAT'S THE BIGGEST challenge in the world? Climate change? Economic disparity? Species extinction? A Western billionaire will likely say population growth. A lot of well-off people in North America and Europe would agree. But is it true?

It's worth considering, especially in light of the fact that, somewhere in the world, the seven-billionth person was recently born. In my lifetime, the human population has more than tripled. (I know I'm guilty of contributing to the boom.) But is overpopulation really the problem it's being made out to be? And if so, what can we do about it?

First, supporting more people on a finite planet with finite resources is a serious challenge. But in a world where hunger and obesity are both epidemic, reproduction rates can't be the main problem. And when we look at issues that are often blamed on overpopulation, we see that over-consumption by the most privileged is a greater factor in rampant environmental destruction and resource depletion.

I once asked the great ecologist E.O. Wilson how many people the planet could sustain indefinitely. He responded, "If you want to live like North Americans, 200 million." North Americans, Europeans, Japanese, and Australians, who make up 20 per cent of the world's population, are consuming more than 80 per cent of the world's resources. We are the major predators and despoilers of the planet, and so we blame the problem on overpopulation. Keep in mind, though, that most environmental devastation is not directly caused by individuals or households, but by corporations driven more by profits than human needs.

The non-profit organization Global Footprint Network calculated the area of land and water the world's human population needs to produce the resources it consumes and to absorb carbon dioxide emissions. If it takes a year or less for nature to regenerate the amount we use in a year, that's sustainable. But they found it takes 1.5 years to replace what we take in a year. That means we are using up our basic biological capital rather than living on the interest, and this has been going on since the 1980s.

As people in developing countries demand more of the bounty and products we take for granted, environmental impacts are bound to increase. The best way to confront these problems is to reduce waste and consumption, find cleaner energy sources, and support other countries in finding ways to develop that are more sustainable than the ways we've employed—to learn from our mistakes. Stabilizing or decreasing population growth will help, but research shows it's not the biggest factor. A United Nations report, "State of World Population 2011," concludes that even zero population growth won't have a huge impact on global warming.

But, just as it's absurd to rely on economies based on constant growth on a finite planet, it can't be sustainable to have a human population that continues to increase exponentially. So, is there any good news? Well, population growth is slowing down. According to the UN report, the average number of children per woman has gone from 6 to 2.5 over the past 60 years. Research shows the best way to stabilize and reduce population growth is through greater protection and respect for women's rights, better access to birth control, widespread education about sex and reproduction, and redistribution of wealth.

But wealthy conservatives who overwhelmingly identify population growth as the biggest problem are often the same people who oppose measures that may slow the rate of growth. This has been especially true in the U.S., where corporate honchos and the politicians who support them fight against environmental protection and against sex education and better access to birth control, not to mention redistribution of wealth.

Population, environmental, and social-justice issues are inextricably linked. Giving women more rights over their own bodies, providing equal opportunity for them to participate in society, and making education and contraception widely available will help stabilize population growth and create numerous other benefits. Reducing economic disparity—between rich and poor individuals and nations—will lead to better allocation of resources. But it's clear that confronting serious environmental problems will take more than just slowing population growth.

Imagine a brighter twenty-first century

IN OUR SHORT time on Earth, we humans have emerged from a chaotic world, imposing order and meaning in myriad ways, imagining the world into being. That was our great gift. As we move through the second decade of the twenty-first century, will we prove ourselves to be imaginative beings capable of creating a better world?

Our challenge is to imagine a world where our wealth is in human relations and where we learn to live in balance with the rest of nature. By imagining a future, we can make it happen—as we always have. If we continue, though, to set human borders and the economy as our highest priorities, we will never come to grips with the destructiveness of our activities and institutions.

In imagining a better future, we must open ourselves to the idea of change. And we'd do well to remember that people with vision have been overturning outmoded ways of thinking and acting throughout our brief history on this earth—often in the face of great resistance. It wasn't long ago that people in countries such as the U.S. believed slavery was an economic necessity and that abolishing it would destroy the economy and the way of life of its "free" citizens.

When it comes to the cost and the speed of acting in our own best interests, consider how quickly the U.S. was able to build its space program after the Russians launched *Sputnik 1* in 1957. In putting tremendous energy, thought, and resources into getting people onto the moon, the U.S. also sparked innovations such as twenty-four-hour television news channels, cellphones, and GPS navigation.

On the environmental front, world leaders came together in Montreal in 1987 to confront the effect humans were having on the ozone layer with our use of chlorofluorocarbons. The international treaty they signed used trade sanctions and incentives to get countries to phase out the use of chemicals that were contributing to the depletion of the ozone layer. And that agreement allowed developing countries to take longer to phase out CFCs because the industrialized world had disproportionately contributed to the problem.

We really do have to think big—to imagine what a future that offers the most good to the most people and to all life on this planet would look like. Obviously, reducing poverty, conflict, and human-rights abuses is paramount. Environmental problems exacerbate those issues and so must also be dealt with. Part of the problem is that many of our political leaders are stuck in the mindset that constant economic growth is essential.

For example, consider what Canadian prime minister Stephen Harper said in a speech to South Korea's National Assembly in late 2009: "Without the wealth that comes from growth, the environmental threats, the developmental challenges, and the peace and security issues facing the world will be exponentially more difficult to deal with." But with constant growth comes depletion of and increasing competition for scarce resources, as well as more waste; in other words, increased environmental threats, developmental challenges, and peace and security issues. Constant growth is just not possible in a finite world with finite resources. Our focus on constant economic growth also leads to some bizarre anomalies. War and natural disasters, for example, can contribute to economic growth by creating employment and resource-use activity.

In thinking beyond these artificial parameters that humans have set (and remember, they were set only during the middle of the twentieth century), we can imagine a more sustainable way of living, as York University economist Peter Victor has done in his excellent book *Managing Without Growth: Slower by Design, Not Disaster*. As Victor points out, we can't change overnight, but by imagining a future in which humans live within the earth's capacity to provide for our ongoing needs, we can steer ourselves in the right direction.

Once we have imagined this better future, we can get serious about solving the challenges we have created with our now outmoded ways of thinking. Issues such as climate change, mass extinctions of plant and animal species, pollution and toxic chemicals in the environment, water shortages, and more require scientific and political solutions—along with the efforts and support of citizens throughout the world.

We're well into the twenty-first century. It's time we started thinking and acting like responsible twenty-first-century citizens. It's time to imagine what we really can be.

At home with nature

LIFE IS BELIEVED to have arisen on Earth some four billion years ago. DNA probes reveal that humans originated as a species in Africa some 150,000 years ago, which makes us evolutionary infants. For most of our brief time here, we understood that we were deeply embedded in and utterly dependent on nature for our survival and well-being. That reality hasn't changed, but our perception of it has.

For most of our existence, we were nomadic hunter-gatherers, following useful plants and animals through the seasons. Our ecological footprint (the amount of land and water required to fulfill our needs) was slight because when you have to carry everything you own, you tend to lug only the bare necessities. People understood and were grateful for nature's abundance and generosity.

About ten thousand years ago, the agricultural revolution signalled a monumental shift in human existence. By deliberately planting and growing food, we could settle in one place and establish roots. Civilizations rose and fell relatively rapidly in evolutionary time, but until the past century, most people lived in rural communities and were involved in growing food.

Farmers watch the seasons carefully. They understand the relationship between winter snow and summer moisture, and they know which plants and insects are beneficial and which are pests. Nature is a dominant reality for farmers, and because so many people were connected to farming in 1900, it was a dominant reality for the world.

In the twentieth century, humankind underwent a profound transformation. From 1900 to 2000, the world's population grew fourfold to six billion people, and the number of cities with a population of more than a million exploded by a factor of thirty to more than four hundred. More than 80 per cent of people in industrialized nations and more than half of the earth's total population now live in cities. This has resulted in a corresponding change in our relationship with nature.

This generation of children spends less time outdoors than any generation in human history. Why are we surprised? Today, a person living in an air-conditioned apartment in New York, Toronto, Sydney, or any other large city can take an elevator to the basement parking lot and drive an air-conditioned car to a garage in a downtown building to work all day in an air-conditioned office. Shopping, eating, and recreation can all be done within interconnected buildings, so there's no need to go outside for days.

I once hosted a television series in which we filmed ten- to twelve-year-old city kids in different locations. For one show, we took a boy and girl to a farm outside of Toronto, where for two days we gathered eggs, milked cows, fed pigs, and rode horses. On the third day, we took the kids to a slaughterhouse where the twelve-year-old boy was upset to learn that hamburgers and wieners were made from the muscles of an animal! City kids often don't know the source of electricity or tap water or the destination of a flushed toilet or garbage on the curb.

Nature is the ultimate source of our water and electricity, and nature absorbs our waste. But in our globalized world, we believe the economy takes precedence over nature, a notion that a provincial environment minister reinforced when he chastised me, saying, "We can't afford to protect the environment if we don't have a strong, growing economy." We hear it in the many arguments that our efforts to reduce greenhouse gas emissions, though necessary, must not inhibit the economy. But the economy is a human invention, whereas nature is what all life depends on. In elevating economics above everything else, we ignore the reality that we live within and make a living from the finite confines of the biosphere.

Nothing within a finite world can grow indefinitely; there are limits. If we are to find a truly sustainable future, we have to put the eco back into economics.

Anti-greenies are stuck in the past

ENVIRONMENTALISTS WON'T be happy until we're living in caves and scrounging for roots and berries. At least, that's what I hear over and over again. The people who say this would have you believe that those of us who care about the earth and its future are neoprimitives who don't believe in modern ways.

Many people before us developed complex societies over hundreds or thousands of years of cultural evolution, and many developed a far more sophisticated understanding of how their food, energy, and other needs affected the ecosystem they relied on than is typically displayed in our own technological society. And so we may have some lessons to learn from our ancestors about our place on this earth. Many people seem to have forgotten, for example, that we are a part of nature, and not beings that stand outside or above it. Valuing these aspects of traditional societies isn't about an atavistic wish to return to "primitive" life; it's about recognizing facets of a more rational way of living.

Most environmentalists I know are looking to the future—a future in which modern and clean technology will help get us out of the environmental and economic jams we're in. We believe that innovations in areas such as solar, wind, geothermal, and tidal power—along with advanced ways of thinking about our relationship with nature—will lead us to a more just and sane path than the one we're on.

Our earliest advances were based on burning wood or dung for fuel. Now we're still using our paleolithic trick: burning decayed organic materials in the form of fossil fuels. Isn't it time we moved on? We are far too numerous—and the impacts of our actions far too great—to keep on acting like cavemen. It seems to me that those who criticize us, the anti-environmentalists, are the ones who want to turn their backs on their future so that they can just go on burning stuff.

Our history is one of change, of coming up with new ideas and new technologies to meet the challenges of allocating resources to growing populations. As environmentalists, we embrace change for the better. But our critics want us to remain stuck in a time that has no future. They reject progress, arguing that we should keep on our destructive way, with outmoded technologies and energy sources. They reject the research of close to 98 per cent of the world's climate scientists, as well as numerous scientific institutions, which shows humans are contributing to rapidly increasing global average temperatures that threaten our future on this finite planet. Many of those who reject this overwhelming scientific evidence do so out of self-interest. The lucrative fossil-fuel industries and their associated lobby groups have invested a lot of time and money into campaigns to stall progress by raising doubt and fear.

These tactics have had an effect. Many people do fear change, and it's often easier to hold on to what you have— even if you know it isn't working—than to embrace new ideas. But beyond the scientific predictions, it's getting more difficult every day to deny the very real and immediate impacts of climate change. Environmental damage from climate change is already killing 300,000 people a year, with an economic impact of $125 billion a year.

A better world for us, our children, and our grandchildren is possible. Just as we're seeing evidence of the damage caused by climate change today, we're also seeing innovative ideas being applied to the problems. Many scientists, economists, environmentalists, business people, and citizens are proposing and implementing solutions. Their work is not only offering hope in the face of the catastrophic effects of climate change, it's also offering hope for faltering economies by ushering in new technologies to replace the jobs and technologies that are becoming obsolete as supplies of polluting fossil fuels become scarce. But the longer we put off fully embracing these solutions the more difficult we will make life for ourselves.

We can continue to burn things until there is nothing left to burn, and we can continue to allow fossil-fuel interests to spew pollution into the air without cost, but where will that leave us? Maybe scrounging for roots and berries and huddling in caves for shelter.

How to become an environmentalist

YOUNG PEOPLE OFTEN ask me what they have to do to be environmentalists. They want to make a difference. My answer is, "Follow your heart. Do what you love most and pursue it with passion." You see, environmentalism isn't a profession or discipline; it's a way of seeing our place in the world. It's recognizing that we live on a planet where everything, including us, is exquisitely interconnected with and interdependent on everything else.

Life-giving water moves from ocean to air to land, across the globe, linking all life through the hydrologic cycle. Every breath we take contains oxygen from every plant on land and in the sea, as well as whatever issues from every factory chimney and vehicle on Earth. The web of all living things constantly partakes of and cleanses, replenishes, and restores air, water, soil, and energy. In this way of seeing the world, we are not only recipients of nature's most vital gifts—we are participants in her cycles.

Whatever we thoughtlessly toss or deliberately dump into our surroundings doesn't simply vanish or dilute away. Our use of air, water, and soil as garbage dumps means that those emissions and pollutants move through the biosphere, ecosystems, habitats, and eventually our own bodies and cells. Environmentalism is recognition of this. We need all people—plumbers, teachers, doctors, carpenters, garage mechanics, business people, artists, scientists—to see and understand the world that way because once we "get it," we treat our surroundings in a radically different way, with the respect that we should have toward our own bodies and loved ones.

For most of human existence, we were hunter-gatherers who understood how deeply embedded in and utterly dependent on nature we were. Until we underwent the massive transformation from agrarian life to big-city dwelling, people knew that we were part of nature and needed nature for survival. We watched the skies for hints of a change in weather or for the first sighting of migrating birds. We welcomed the appearance of buds on the bushes, the first signs of spring thaw, or the indicators that winter was on its way.

We now live in a shattered world, with torrents of information assaulting us from every angle. Headlines may scream of the aftermath of a hockey playoff or a devastating tornado in the southern U.S., and then trumpet Oprah's last TV program and another sex scandal. And then we hear of floods in Pakistan or Manitoba, forest fires raging in northern Alberta, thinning sea ice in the Arctic, retreating glaciers, and drought in rainforests.

Reports about floods and droughts and sea ice and climate change get sandwiched between clips about scandals and celebrities, and so we view them as isolated events. An environmental perspective would consider the possibility that many of the events are connected to an underlying cause. Such a perspective would help us get to the root of problems rather than trying to stamp out brushfires without identifying the source of the conflagration.

We tend to think of environmentalists as folks concerned about nature or an endangered species or threatened ecosystem. Environmentalists are accused of caring more for spotted owls or trees than people and jobs. That's absurd. In seeing a world of interconnections, we understand that people are at the heart of a global ecocrisis and that genuine sustainability means also dealing with issues of hunger and poverty, of inequity and lack of justice, of terrorism, genocide, and war, because as long as these issues confront humanity, sustainability will be a low priority.

In our interconnected world, all of these issues are a part of the unsustainable path we are on. If we want to find solutions, we have to look at the big picture.

Humans may have loaded
the bases, but nature bats last

HUMANITY IS FACING a challenge unlike any we've
ever had to confront. We are in an unprecedented period
of change. Exponential growth is causing an already
huge human population to double in shorter and shorter
time periods.

When I was born, in 1936, just over two billion people
lived on the planet. It's astounding that the population has
increased more than threefold within my lifetime. That
staggering growth has been accompanied by even steeper
increases in technological innovation, consumption, and a
global economy that exploits the entire planet as a source
of raw materials and a dumping ground for toxic emissions and waste. We have become a new kind of biological
force that is altering the physical, chemical, and biological
properties of the planet on a geological scale. Indeed, Nobel
Prize-winning chemist Paul Crutzen has suggested that the
current geologic period should be called the Anthropocene
epoch to reflect our new status as a global force—and a lot of
scientists agree.

As noted in an article in the *Economist,* "Welcome to
the Anthropocene," we are altering the earth's carbon cycle,
which leads to climate change, and we have sped up the
nitrogen cycle by more than 150 per cent, which has led to
acid rain, ozone depletion, and coastal dead zones, among
other impacts. We have also replaced wilderness with farms
and cities, which has had a huge effect on biodiversity.

On top of that, according to the *Economist,* a "single
engineering project, the Syncrude mine in the Athabasca
tar sands, involves moving thirty billion tonnes of earth—
twice the amount of sediment that flows down all the rivers

in the world in a year." As for those global sediment flows, the article goes on to point out that they have been cut by nearly a fifth, eroding the earth's deltas "faster than they can be replenished," thanks to the almost fifty thousand large dams built in the world over the past half-century.

We now occupy every continent and are exploring every nook and cranny of the earth for new resources. The collective ecological impact of humanity far exceeds the planet's capacity to sustain us indefinitely at this level of activity. Studies suggest it now takes 1.5 years for nature to restore what humanity removes of its renewable resources in a year, and this deficit spending has been going on since the 1980s.

For the first time in human history, we have to respond as a single species to crises of our own making. Until now, this kind of unified effort happened only in science fiction when space aliens invaded Earth. In those stories, world leaders overcame human divisions to work together against the common enemy. Now, as comic strip character Pogo said in the 1970s (appropriately, on a poster created for Earth Day): "We have met the enemy and he is us." Humans have long been able to affect the environment, but never before on such a scale. In the past, even people with primitive tools and weapons had impacts on local flora and fauna, as Tim Flannery outlined in *The Future Eaters* and Jared Diamond described in *Collapse*. Diminishing resources forced people to come to grips with the need to sustain their resources or to move in search of new opportunities.

The only way to come to grips with the crises and find solutions is to understand that we are biological creatures, with an absolute need for clean air, clean water, clean food and soil, clean energy, and biodiversity. Capitalism, communism, democracy, free enterprise, corporations, economies, and markets do not alter those basic needs. After all, those are human constructs, not forces of nature. Similarly, the borders we draw around our property, cities, states, and countries mean nothing to nature.

All the hopes that meetings such as the Earth Summit in Rio de Janeiro in 1992 and the climate conferences in Kyoto in 1997, Copenhagen in 2009, and Cancun in 2010 would help us resolve major ecological challenges will be dashed as long as we continue to put economic and political considerations above our most fundamental biological, social, and spiritual needs. We humans may be heavy hitters, but we must remember that nature bats last.

Our perceptual filters shape the world

IF PRESENTED WITH the autopsied brains of an array of people, no expert would be able to distinguish from the brains' anatomy or neurocircuitry the gender, religion, or socio-economic class of the cadavers. Because we are members of one species, our brains, neurons, and sensory organs are similar in structure and chemistry. But if you were to ask both men and women about love and family, Israelis and Palestinians about Gaza, Catholics and Protestants in Belfast about British occupation, Republicans and Democrats about Karl Rove, and Shias, Sunnis, and Kurds about U.S. troops, you'd think the respondents came from different planets.

What this demonstrates is that we learn to see the world through perceptual lenses formed by heredity, upbringing, personal experiences, religion, socio-economic differences, and so on. Even though we detect our surroundings in the same way through eyes, ears, nose, skin, and tongue, our brains filter that incoming information so that it "makes sense" according to our individual values and beliefs. This creates huge dissonance between fossil-fuel executives, environmentalists, and politicians when we discuss an issue like climate change.

I was reminded of how acutely our values affect our ability to see things when I accompanied ethnobotanist Wade Davis to a remote village at the foot of a large mountain in Peru. Wade told me that the villagers regard that mountain as an "apu," or god, and believe that as long as it casts its shadow on the community, it will shape their lives. "Compare the way a child in this village treats that mountain with a Canadian kid in the Rockies who is taught a mountain is full of gold and other valuable minerals," Wade said. The way we perceive the world shapes the way we treat it.

I have thought of Wade's story often. How differently we would behave if we thought of a forest as a sacred grove instead of timber and pulp, of a river as the veins of the land rather than a source of irrigation or power, of soil as a complex community of organisms and not dirt, of other species as our evolutionary kin rather than resources, of our house as our home instead of property.

Most of our battles over environmental issues revolve around the differences in how we perceive and define the problem. While filming a special program on forestry for *The Nature of Things* in the 1990s, we arranged to interview loggers working in a cut block near Ucluelet on Vancouver Island. When we arrived and set up the camera, the loggers came out of the forest and began to cuss me out as an environmentalist who was threatening their jobs. The confrontation made for good television, but I was frustrated at our inability to find common ground. Finally I told them, "I worked as a carpenter for eight years, and to this day, I love working with wood. No environmentalist I know is against logging. We just want to be sure that your children and grandchildren will be able to log forests as rich as the ones you're working in now."

Immediately, one of the men replied that he'd never let his kids go into logging. "There won't be any trees left!" he said. And there it was. Those men knew that they were cutting the trees down in a way that ensured there would be no harvestable timber for future generations of loggers, but they saw the trees as the way to put food on the table day after day and make the house and car payments at the end of the month.

How can we resolve such differences in perspective? I don't know, but I'm sure that the challenge has to do with what's locked inside our skulls. I have spent more than forty years trying to use the electronic media to inform and educate, but I continue to be flabbergasted by the strength of those perceptual filters.

We have to find ways of overcoming those blocks so that we can begin to agree on some basic principles. We are not outside or on top of the web of living things; we are deeply embedded in it and utterly dependent on it for our survival and well-being. Without that understanding, we will continue on our destructive rampage.

It's easy being green

I ONCE READ an article about a woman in Spokane, Washington, who didn't like phosphate-free dishwashing detergents. Phosphate-containing detergents are banned in Spokane County because of their negative impact on the environment, so the woman drove forty-five minutes to Idaho where phosphate detergents were still sold. The article also noted that the woman had a five-year-old daughter. I was astounded.

People often argue that protecting the environment will require too many sacrifices. Is this what they mean? That they would risk their children's futures because they can't be bothered to rinse their dishes before putting them into the dishwasher? Phosphates are added to cleaning products because they help cut grease and get rid of food particles on dishes. But they also have enormous negative impacts on rivers, streams, and lakes. By fertilizing the waters, phosphates can cause massive algae blooms that starve the water of oxygen and choke aquatic ecosystems, killing fish, amphibians, insects, and plants. Phosphates have been banned from laundry detergents in most places for a number of years now, but consumers have resisted moves to ban them from dishwashing detergents.

The article notes that the Spokane River is one of the most endangered in the U.S. and that phosphate pollution from the county's main wastewater treatment plant has been reduced by 14 per cent since the dishwasher-detergent law was passed in July 2011. But apparently this woman doesn't care if the river is devoid of life when her daughter grows up—as long as her dishes are spot-free!

The woman claims to be "environmentally conscious." I guess she means that she cares about the environment only when it is convenient for her. This is a good example of the kind of challenges faced by people who really do care about the environment and the future. Part of the problem may be that some people can't really relate their own behaviour to the consequences. Think of parents with asthmatic children who continue to smoke in the house or drive suvs. Others are simply not willing to make even the smallest sacrifices when it comes to protecting the environment. Yet, for the most part, no great sacrifices are required.

I often hear from people who think it would be difficult to get up a bit earlier and expend a bit more energy to cycle to work instead of drive, for example. But they soon find that the benefits of cycling—from getting in better shape to enjoying the outside world—far outweigh any negative consequences. It's more about changing the way we think than about giving something up. If we take a broader, more long-range view of things, we see that we usually gain more than we lose when we make changes in our lives to protect our surroundings.

We see the same kind of resistance to things like a carbon tax. Never mind that market forces play a far greater role in fuel-price increases than a carbon tax ever will! People see that they might have to pay a few pennies more at the gas pump or for home-heating bills and they immediately cry that they will have to give up their cars and freeze in their homes during winter. But we see immediate and long-term benefits from putting a price on carbon. People find ways to conserve energy, companies invest in technologies that use renewable energy, and we end up with less pollution and fewer emissions that contribute to global warming.

We live in consumer societies, especially here in North America. We've become convinced that we have to keep replacing our goods with newer and "better," often over-packaged, products. We dispose of things even before they have broken down. And the world suffers for it. We can lead lives that are even more fulfilling on a cleaner planet where more people have access to clean air, water, and food. All it takes is some imagination and some forward thinking. If we really cared about our world and about our children and grandchildren, we would be willing to make some sacrifices to make the world a better, healthier place. But in most cases, the sacrifices are as illusory as some of the benefits we think we are deriving from our rampant consumerism.

Life-altering planetary experience

INSURANCE COMPANIES, politicians, and business people often use the expressions "natural disaster" or "act of God" to deflect responsibility for events beyond our control. Today, human activity and technology have become so powerful that we are contributing to what were once natural disasters. Hurricanes, tornadoes, freak storms, floods, droughts, pest outbreaks, heat waves, and even earthquakes are occurring with greater frequency and intensity than ever. Some of this can be traced to human activity. Greenhouse gases, immense dams, and deep oil and water wells can all affect natural forces.

Since life first appeared on Earth some four billion years ago, it has played a critical role in altering the physical and chemical properties of the planet. For the first couple of billion years, it was a microbial world, yet those microscopic organisms acted with other forces to break down rock. Over time, this process reduced mountains and boulders to stones, gravel, and dust, releasing minerals and creating soils from the carcasses of organisms.

Life is thought to have evolved in oceans. Here, carbon from the atmosphere dissolved in the water to form carbonaceous shells that offered protection for some life forms. When these died, they sank to the ocean floor where eventually their accumulated shells were pressurized into limestone. Limestone is rock, created by life, which stores carbon in the ground.

As life forms evolved, they grew bigger, in part by incorporating and storing water. In doing so, they became a critical part of the hydrologic cycle, the process whereby water evaporates, forms clouds, and rains back onto the earth in an endless loop. Organisms could take up dissolved minerals and trace chemicals from the water and release them with their own wastes. After plants evolved into trees on land, they became efficient at sucking water from soil and transpiring most of it into the air to affect weather and climate.

The evolution of photosynthesis was a huge biological breakthrough, enabling Earth's life to capture vast amounts of energy in the form of sunlight. During photosynthesis, plants release oxygen. Over millions of years, this process reduced the amount of carbon dioxide in the atmosphere while creating oxygen-rich air that animals like us depend on.

So for billions of years, the web of life has played a crucial role in changing the physical, chemical, and biological features of the planet. Life was not just opportunistic in exploiting physical and chemical opportunities; living organisms interacted with and changed the planet's earth, water, and air—or biosphere. But it took vast periods of time and millions of diverse species. In all that time, no single species was able to rapidly alter the properties of Earth on a geological scale—until now.

Humans appeared during the last moment of evolutionary time, perhaps 150,000 years ago. For most of our brief existence, we were tribal animals who didn't even know whether other humans lived on the other side of an ocean, desert, or mountain. We only had to worry about our own territory and tribe. Suddenly, we have become a geological force, the most prolific mammal on the planet, endowed with powerful technologies, impelled by an insatiable appetite for stuff, and supplied by a global economy. Taken together, our numbers, technology, consumption, and global economy have made us a new kind of force on the planet. For the first time, we must ask, "What is the collective impact of seven billion human beings?" As we begin to answer that question, we are left with the extreme difficulty of responding to global threats that our own activity has caused.

Many people harbour an understandable tendency to deny the reality of the crisis in the biosphere. After all, how can puny humans have such a massive impact on this large planet? Some also maintain a conceit that we can manage our way out of the mess, increasingly with heroic interventions of technology. But we've learned from past technologies—nuclear power, DDT, CFCs—that we don't know enough about how the world works to anticipate and minimize unexpected consequences.

The truth is that the only factor or species we can manage on Earth is us. We have no choice but to address the challenge of bringing our cities, energy needs, agriculture, fishing fleets, mines, and so on into balance with the factors that support all life. This crisis can become an opportunity, if we seize it and get on with finding solutions.

Brain over brawn is the key to survival

MANY PEOPLE SAY the late George Wald was the greatest lecturer in Harvard's history. He was certainly the best I've heard. George won a Nobel Prize in 1967 for his work on the biochemical basis of colour vision. He and I became friends in the 1970s because we shared a common concern about the misapplication of science, especially during the war in Vietnam. George once captivated me with a story he told:

For close to 150 million years, dinosaurs dominated the planet, and they were impressive. They were huge animals, armed with weapons like spikes on their tails, giant claws, and razor-sharp teeth. They were covered with armour plates. They seemed invincible, and when they roamed the earth, other creatures fled in terror. But they had a fatal flaw: a tiny brain in relation to their body size. Despite their impressive traits, they disappeared—victims, in part, of their low brain-to-brawn ratio.

About 64 million years after the dinosaurs went extinct, a beautiful animal appeared on the plains of Africa. This animal stood upright and walked on two legs, and its skin was free of fur. Unlike the plentiful wildebeest, this animal was rare. It wasn't as big as a hippo. It wasn't even as fast as an elephant. It wasn't as strong as a chimpanzee, and it couldn't see like an eagle, smell like a dog, or hear like a gazelle. But those first beautiful humans were endowed with the highest brain-to-brawn ratio ever achieved, and in only 150,000 years, they had spread to every continent on Earth. Humans eventually outnumbered other mammals on the planet. Their high brain-to-brawn ratio served them well as they learned to domesticate plants and animals and to live in environments as varied as Arctic tundra, deserts, coral atolls, mountain slopes, wetlands, and forests of every kind.

But then they invented guns and cannons, and their brain-to-brawn ratio fell. They got into cars, tanks, and planes and dropped napalm and nuclear bombs. And with each innovation, the brain-to-brawn ratio sank toward that of the dinosaurs.

I love George's story because it encapsulates much of our dilemma. The human brain was the critical factor that more than compensated for our lack of physical and sensory abilities. We had a vast memory, we were observant and curious, and we were creative. In the past, our innovations such as the needle, bow and arrow, and pottery had huge repercussions but took centuries to evolve into the culture.

Agriculture was the big shift that released us from being nomadic hunter-gatherers to farmers and village dwellers. Then the Industrial Revolution heralded a massive change. In only two centuries, people were able to harness the cheap, portable energy of fossil fuels to create machines of incredible power. In the movie *Avatar,* the giant robots have no heads, a symbol of what we have become as a species. We have acquired vast technological power but far too little of the brainpower or wisdom needed to use that power well.

Consider this simple example. When New Zealand fishermen discovered a fish called orange roughy in deep-sea waters, they thought they had hit a bonanza. Technology to fish the deep sea—radar, sonar, GPS, freezers, giant nets—enabled them to exploit the abundant fish in massive numbers. Despite the fact that these were a new target species about which virtually nothing was known, the animals were taken in vast quantities. It's called "harvesting" but it was really a "mining" operation. Only years later did we learn these fish live for more than a hundred years and grow and mature far more slowly than inshore species.

When was the last time you ate orange roughy? They have been nearly wiped out all around the globe because our technology was too powerful in relation to our knowledge. We didn't consider our limitations, which should have caused us to be far more cautious and conservative.

The technology meant that our brain-to-brawn ratio sank toward a level closer to that of the dinosaurs.

Technology can provide great benefits, but unless we learn to use our heads in applying our technologies, we will also go the way of the dinosaurs.

Fables from old times have meaning for our times

WHEN WADING THROUGH the words of pundits and the babble of political posturing, I can't help but think of some of the simple truths we learned as children. Remember those stories from Aesop, Hans Christian Andersen, and the Grimm brothers that enthralled us while imparting powerful messages? Two childhood fables seem particularly important today.

Once upon a time, a couple owned a goose that laid a golden egg every day. They became very rich but were not content with a single egg a day. In their greed, they killed the goose to get at the eggs inside. Of course, they found the goose had guts like any other goose, and they ended up with nothing.

I thought of that story while working on a *Nature of Things* program on the destruction of the Amazon rainforest. In the 1980s, Brazil's government encouraged people to move to the Amazon to make a living or a fortune. "Land without people for people without land" was how the government promoted it. So one of the largest, most complex, and irreplaceable ecosystems on the planet has been logged, flooded, mined, and burned for decades as Brazilians seek their fabled El Dorado, the city of gold. But, as in the fairy tale about the goose, El Dorado is the forest, not the resources being exploited by destroying it.

Many see the destructive activities in South America as a response to poverty. If that's true, what's our excuse? In North America, we have demolished the bulk of our original forests through the unsustainable practice of clear-cut logging. Across the country, one logging community after another has gone from boom to bust as forests have been cut down. The golden eggs were the economic benefits of logging, which could have been obtained year after year, as long as the goose—the forest—was healthy.

Over and over, we find ourselves rushing to get more eggs. In doing so, we end up losing the goose. We do it in agriculture as we use up the topsoil created over millennia; we do it in fisheries as our increasing technological power allows us to catch more fish faster; and we do it in the northern Alberta tar sands as we tear up boreal ecosystems, pollute the water, and inject massive amounts of greenhouse gas into the atmosphere, all to get more of those eggs. And damn the goose.

I thought of another children's tale while listening to the CBC News's Peter Mansbridge interview Prime Minister Stephen Harper in 2010. The prime minister claimed Canadians were concerned only about the economy and that Canada's possible involvement with torture in Afghanistan was not a serious concern. The prime minister also ignored the massive public demand for leadership on climate change that preceded Copenhagen. The tale that comes to mind is the story of the emperor who wore no clothes.

Long ago, a vain emperor was overly concerned about his appearance. Two crafty weavers promised to make him a fine outfit from material that could not be seen by those who were stupid or unfit for their position. When the weavers pretended to display samples, the emperor couldn't admit he was unable to see them, for that would be an admission of incompetence or stupidity. His courtiers and ministers were likewise unable to admit they saw nothing. When the weavers came with the finished outfit, everyone oohed and aahed. Putting on the imaginary clothes, the emperor paraded outside so that the public could admire him and his new attire. Everyone in the crowd, enthralled by the status of the king and bowed by their desire to be seen as clever and fashionable, remained silent. Only a child, innocent of the claims of the weavers, pointed out the obvious and said: "The emperor has no clothes."

We are living in a time when ecological degradation is occurring everywhere. B.C.'s northern forests have turned red, victims of mountain pine beetles no longer killed by winters that have become too warm. Farmers know harvest time is later, birders report birds migrating north two weeks earlier and departing weeks later than normal, competitive skiers tell us European meets are being cancelled for lack of snow. Glaciers are receding, Arctic ice is melting— the list is long. But where the emperor and his sycophantic subjects are blinded by vanity, we are prevented from seeing by the cloak of economics and politics.

Let's throw off the blinders and see the world as any child can.

What do you want for Christmas?

IN MUCH OF the Western world, the December festive season has become little more than a celebration of excess and conspicuous consumption. We run around in malls like maniacs as we count the "shopping days" till Christmas, searching for the perfect gifts for everyone we know. We stop briefly to gorge ourselves on turkey and pie, and on the day after Christmas, we rush back to the malls to see what kind of deals we can get.

Now, there's nothing wrong with offering gifts to friends and family, and there's certainly nothing wrong with celebrating those connections with wonderful feasts. Although I'm not a Christian, I love the rituals and family time that come with the holiday season. But it's gotten out of hand. It may be good for the economy, but is it good for our mental health—and is it good for the environment? What's really important as we celebrate this time of year when longer nights give way to longer days? I had a chance to think about some of these things as I prepared to give what has been called my Legacy Lecture in Vancouver in late 2009 and to accept a Right Livelihood Award in Sweden.

In writing the speeches, I reflected on the values I have learned during my time on Earth. It reaffirmed my belief that our most important need as social animals is love. Everything else flows from this—our commitment to protect the environment so that our own lives and those of our children and grandchildren will be healthier; our recognition that we are all connected to each other and to the natural world through the air we breathe, the water we drink, and the food we eat; and our belief that all the world's people have a right to justice and freedom.

Whether it's for holy days or the winter solstice—or both—this time of year offers the chance to reflect and to be with people we love. For many people, the solstice symbolizes renewal and rebirth. We should take advantage of this by using the time wisely. And maybe the wisest use of our time is not to run around shopping and stressing, but rather just to spend it with our loved ones and to consider what we can do for this earth that gives us so much.

To start, we can make the holiday season itself greener. Gift giving is a tradition with tremendous symbolic value, but rather than giving each other gadgets and gewgaws that end up in the landfill in less than a year, we should put some thought into gifts that are meaningful and that are preferably made locally and made to last—unless the gift is food or drink, of course, even though some of the Christmas cake I've seen seems like it could last forever! How about recycling something that we've already used, like a good book? You could also consider gifts offered by conservation groups or other non-profit organizations that help advance worthy causes, or give a donation in the gift recipient's name. To me, one of our most important rituals is giving gifts to others who are not as well off as us, either at home or in poorer countries.

Gift wrap and cards also have an impact on the environment. If you must wrap your gifts, save a tree and use recycled paper, gift wrap from previous years, or even newspaper. Use cards that are made from post-consumer recycled paper—or send e-cards. You can also tear off the fronts of old cards to reuse them, or even forego an envelope and make them into postcards. The David Suzuki Foundation's Queen of Green, Lindsay Coulter, suggests cutting old cards into cool holiday shapes to make excellent gift tags.

Speaking of trees, I'm often asked whether it's better to use real or artificial Christmas trees. A life-cycle assessment study conducted by sustainability research firm ellipsos inc. found that real trees are better for the environment overall than fake trees. In Vancouver, the CarbonSync organization will even rent you a potted tree that they will deliver and then pick up after Christmas and plant, with some of the proceeds going to the Burns Bog Conservation Society.

I'm sure we can all think of ways to make the Christmas season a celebration not just of family and friends but of the wonderful Earth that is our home.

Everything is illuminated

DECEMBER HAS traditionally been a time for people in the northern hemisphere to celebrate light. The nights get longer until December 21, when the North Pole is tilted farthest from the sun, and then light returns as the days start to grow longer.

Chanukah is a Jewish celebration of light. Christianity celebrates the birth of Jesus, who is often represented as light. Our word *yule* comes from the pre-Christian Scandinavian tradition of lighting fires to celebrate the warmth and light of the returning sun. Many indigenous people have also celebrated the shift to longer days and the impending rebirth of life when plants would spring up and animals would emerge from hibernation.

We get almost all of our light—and energy—from the sun. Most of it is in the form of visible light, but some is higher-energy ultraviolet light and some is lower-energy infrared light. This light gets converted to other forms of energy through a variety of fascinating processes. People have been using energy to create light in the same way as the sun—with heat—for centuries. From the fire of torches and candles to the incandescent light bulb, we have found ways to bring both light and warmth into our lives.

Light is produced by energizing atoms. The most basic way to do this is to heat the atoms. At low temperatures, you get red, but the more atoms you energize, the brighter the light gets. The brightest is white, which is not a colour at all but is made up of many different colour frequencies.

Colour itself is created through our perception of light waves at different frequencies. We see colour either as light waves emitted from an object at a particular frequency or as the waves that are reflected back when the object absorbs other frequencies. We see plants as green because chlorophyll pigments absorb light photons in a way that makes the wavelength appear to us as green, and this pigment masks less dominant ones. In the fall, when leaves stop producing these pigments and the chlorophyll breaks down, other pigments are uncovered, appearing as red, orange, and yellow. Plants capture light from the sun and convert it to chemical energy through photosynthesis. And we absorb, store, and convert that energy to power our own cells when we eat the plants or other animals that have eaten the plants.

Hundreds of millions of years ago, some plants and animals retained this energy when they died. Buried and compressed for millennia, their energy concentrated as hydrocarbons to form coal and oil. We burn these materials to release the energy stored within them. We say these fuels are non-renewable because it would take millions of years to create more of them. So fossil fuels are really forms of solar energy, because their power initially came from the sun.

Wind energy is also a function of sunlight. When the sun warms the earth's atmosphere, it creates wind, which can turn turbines to produce electricity.

Energy cannot be created or destroyed; it can only be converted from one form to another. Most of the energy we use today comes from burning fossil fuels. Because the energy has been highly concentrated over millennia, these fuels pack a real punch. For large-scale power generation, the energy is released through heat and converted to electrical energy, and then transported through cables. But this process is inefficient, causes pollution, and contributes to global warming. For example, for every three tonnes of coal burned in a power plant, two are wasted in getting the energy from the coal, converting it to electricity, and transmitting the power to customers.

Whether we are lighting or heating our homes or powering our vehicles, we must find more efficient methods to generate energy—methods that use most of the energy for its intended purpose and that don't create a lot of waste or pollution through procurement, conversion, and transmission. We can also find ways to use less energy.

Part of the solution to our energy-related problems may lie in finding more direct ways to use the sun's energy. And that's something we can all celebrate as we contemplate the sun's return to the northern hemisphere and the warmth, colour, and rebirth it brings with it.

Lessons my father taught me

I LOOK BACK at the world of my childhood, with its shared phone lines, ice boxes, radio soap operas, and lack of television, and it seems like an ancient, lost civilization. And yet the ideas and values I learned as a child seem every bit as important for today's youth, for whom rappers, billionaires, and movie stars are role models.

When I was a boy, my father was a bigger-than-life figure, a wonderful storyteller who enchanted people with his outgoing personality. He was my hero. He took me camping and fishing and instilled in me a love of nature and the outdoors. When he came home from work, he always asked me what I had learned in school, and as I recounted my lessons, he seemed genuinely interested, often amplifying my information or correcting me. I loved those sessions, and I now realize that he was reinforcing my education by making me recount what I had learned.

Dad was my biggest booster, but he was also my harshest critic. When I began working in television, he followed everything I did. More than once when he couldn't follow my narrative, he would call and bawl me out: "If I can't understand what you are saying, how do you expect someone who doesn't know you at all to follow your ideas?" To this day, I think of my father as my audience whenever I prepare a script or write a book.

My mother was the rock-solid foundation of the family. She was the first up in the morning and the last to bed at night, but, unlike Dad, she did it quietly. I understood how important she was only as she developed Alzheimer's disease and I watched Dad struggle to fill her shoes. I begged him to allow me to hire help for him, but he declined. "She gave her all for me," he said, "and it's my turn to pay her back."

Both of my parents are now dead, and in my own dotage I think about the important lessons I want to pass on to my children and grandchildren—and I realize they are the same lessons I got from Dad. I can't help thinking they are not quaint ideas from the past but very modern ones that we need desperately today.

"Respect your elders," he told me. "But Dad," I protested, "Mr. Saita is a fool."

"David," Dad remonstrated, "he has lived a long life and has had experiences and thought about a lot of things you haven't. I know he seems opinionated and stupid, but if you listen, even he can teach you something."

"To do well in Canada as a Japanese-Canadian," he said, "you have to work ten times harder, you must be able to get up and speak extemporaneously, and you must be able to dance." Fortunately, hard work was never an obstacle for me, and I entered oratorical contests for which Dad drilled me in the art of public speaking. I never understood the dancing part and was not successful in that area.

"Whatever you do, do it with gusto. Don't do it in a sloppy, half-hearted way but enthusiastically, whether it's scrubbing the floors, picking cherries, or playing basketball. That's how you get the most out of life."

"We all need money for the necessities in life, but don't run after it as if money makes you a bigger or better man. If someone flashes his fancy new clothes or big car, pity him, because he has gone down the wrong road."

"Live within your means." This important lesson is embodied in the familiar expression, "Save some for a rainy day."

"You must stand up for what you believe in, but be prepared for people to be angry and to disagree. If you want to be liked by everyone, then you will stand for nothing."

"You are what you *do*, not what you *say*." Kids have a different way of saying this in their taunt, "All talk and no action."

My mother also taught me useful homilies, like "Always clean up your own mess," "Be kind to animals," and "Share; don't be greedy."

Today's youth are bombarded with news about the antics of celebrities and rock stars, and they look to them for inspiration, but that's all the more reason to listen to the words of our elders.

A grumpy old man ponders the past

NOW THAT I'VE passed my seventy-fifth birthday, I've been thinking about my children and grandchildren and what lies ahead for them. We trumpet the enormous scientific advances and technological innovations of the twentieth century, but is the world a better place than when I was born?

Reflecting on what we leave to our grandchildren, I have to answer with a resounding no! Yes, things have changed a lot in my lifetime, sometimes for the better. When I was born, there were no transoceanic phone lines, organ transplants, jet planes, satellites, television, oral contraceptives, photocopiers, CDs, computers, antibiotics, cellphones. Today, we have seasonal fruits and vegetables year-round, twenty-four-hour television channels, and bottled water shipped halfway around the world. And stuff! My God, the stuff we can buy. We can choose from more than two hundred brands of breakfast cereals, and last year's cellphones not only seem old fashioned, they're designed to be thrown away. Pills not only offer relief from the horror of erectile dysfunction but can be taken daily to make us ready for action at all times. This is progress?

How quaint my childhood seems today. On hearing me talk about what we didn't have back then, children stare in amazement that anyone can remember such a primitive way of life. "What did you do?" they ask, struggling to imagine a world without television, computers, or cellphones. Yes, mine was an ancient civilization, now extinct.

It's not that I don't appreciate many of the advances. When I was a teenager in the 1950s, I developed pneumonia and was near death when the doctor gave me a shot of penicillin. The next day, I was out of bed running around.

It was truly a miracle drug. My first portable computer in the 1980s allowed me to write and send my columns to the *Globe and Mail* from all over the world. And when my children went away to university in the 1990s, I could stay in touch by email.

Yes, our world now provides a cornucopia of wondrous consumer goods. But at what cost? When I was a child, we spent our time playing in grassy fields, ditches, or creeks. We drank from rivers and lakes and caught and ate fish, without worrying about what chemicals might be in them. When I was a child, the oceans were still rich with marine life, places like the Amazon and Congo were still unexplored ecosystems, and nuclear weapons and the arms race were still to come.

The earth's population has more than tripled since I was born. Each of us now carries dozens of toxic chemicals embedded within us, cancer has become the biggest killer, and we have poisoned our air, water, and soil. The human rush to exploit resources or take over territory has devastated terrestrial and marine plants and animals.

Yes, we leave to our children and grandchildren a world of technological marvels and personal hyperconsumption, but at the expense of community, species diversity, and clean air, water, and soil. I don't remember feeling deprived or bored as a child. My friends were neighbours and our surroundings were rich with biological treasures for us to discover and explore. Almost all of our food was locally grown without the aid of chemicals. And growing up, we were attuned to the impact of weather and climate; we looked forward to the seasons and the changes they brought.

Have I become a grumpy old man who sees only the past as wonderful and decries the modern? I don't think so, but I mourn the passing of a time when community and neighbours were a vital part of social and economic life, a time when nature was still rich. I know we can't change the past, but together we can create a brighter future for our children and grandchildren. We know where the problems lie, and science offers many solutions. Now it's time for action. If I've learned one lesson in my seventy-five years, it's that everyone, including those in government and business, must pitch in if we want to change things for the better.

Acknowledgements

IT TAKES MANY people to make a book like this. It would certainly not have been possible without the amazing dedication, research, ideas, and support of staff at the David Suzuki Foundation. Thanks especially to DSF terrestrial conservation and science program director Faisal Moola, who contributed ideas, research, writing, and perceptive feedback for many of these columns, especially those about species and habitat conservation and natural capital.

Many others have offered ideas, research, and feedback on the columns, including Scott Wallace, Jeffery Young, and Bill Wareham from the marine and freshwater conservation team; Dale Marshall, Ian Bruce, and Tyler Bryant from the climate change and clean energy team; Jode Roberts from communications, and Gail Mainster, who always helps us write more clearly, even when we send her the column a few hours before deadline.

We are incredibly grateful to Rob Sanders, Nancy Flight, and the editors at Greystone Books/D&M, not just for this book but for all the great books they continue to publish on the important topics of our day.

The book is also made possible by the newspaper, magazine, and website editors who share the weekly Science Matters column with their readers and often give those readers a chance to contribute to the conversation through comments and letters.

Thanks most of all to our readers, who are so passionate about these ideas whether they always agree with them or not. A special thank you to those who take the time to respond, either in the media or by sending us letters.

On a personal note, I'd like to thank my co-author, David Suzuki, one of the most honest, caring, and hard-working people I know, for his wonderful writing, and his inspiration, humour, and optimism. I'd also like to thank my son, Luc, who fills me with so much joy and hope and gives me so many reasons to care.

—IH

Index

Other titles from the David Suzuki Foundation and Greystone Books

BY DAVID SUZUKI

- The Legacy: An Elder's Vision for Our Sustainable Future
- The Big Picture: Reflections on Science, Humanity, and a Quickly Changing Planet | with DAVE ROBERT TAYLOR
- David Suzuki's Green Guide | with DAVID R. BOYD
- The David Suzuki Reader
- The Declaration of Interdependence: A Pledge to Planet Earth with TARA CULLIS
- From Naked Ape to Superspecies: Humanity and the Global Eco-Crisis | with HOLLY DRESSEL
- Good News for a Change: How Everyday People Are Helping the Planet | with HOLLY DRESSEL
- More Good News: Real Solutions to the Global Eco-Crisis with HOLLY DRESSEL
- The Sacred Balance: Rediscovering Our Place in Nature with AMANDA MCCONNELL, ADRIENNE MASON
- The Sacred Balance: A Visual Celebration of Our Place in Nature | with AMANDA MCCONNELL
- Tree: A Life Story | with WAYNE GRADY
- When the Wild Comes Leaping Up: Personal Encounters with Nature
- Wisdom of the Elders: Native and Scientific Ways of Knowing about Nature | with PETER KNUDTSON

NATURE PHOTOGRAPHY

- **Arctic Eden:** Journeys through the Changing High Arctic
  JERRY KOBALENKO
- **Beneath Cold Seas:** The Underwater Wilderness of the Pacific
  Northwest | DAVID HALL
- **The Sacred Headwaters:** The Fight to Save the Stikine, Skeena,
  and Nass | WADE DAVIS
- **Wild Prairie:** A Photographer's Personal Journey | JAMES R. PAGE

NATURE WRITING

- **An Enchantment of Birds:** Memories from a Birder's Life
  RICHARD CANNINGS
- **Dark Waters Dancing to a Breeze:** A Literary Companion
  to Rivers and Lakes | ED. WAYNE GRADY
- **Deserts:** A Literary Companion | ED. WAYNE GRADY
- **Gardens:** A Literary Companion | ED. MERILYN SIMONDS
- **Night:** A Literary Companion | ED. MERILYN SIMONDS
- **Northern Wild:** Best Contemporary Canadian Nature Writing
  ED. DAVID R. BOYD
- **A Passion for This Earth:** Writers, Scientists, and Activists
  Explore Our Relationship with Nature and the Environment
  ED. MICHELLE BENJAMIN
- **The Sea:** A Literary Companion | ED. WAYNE GRADY
- **Where the Silence Rings:** A Literary Companion to Mountains
  ED. WAYNE GRADY

CHILDREN'S BOOKS

- **Eco-Fun:** Great Projects, Experiments and Games for a
  Greener Earth | DAVID SUZUKI, KATHY VANDERLINDEN
- **Salmon Forest** | DAVID SUZUKI, SARAH ELLIS
- **There's a Barnyard in My Bedroom** | DAVID SUZUKI
- **You Are the Earth:** Know Your World So You Can Help Make
  It Better | DAVID SUZUKI, KATHY VANDERLINDEN

The David Suzuki Foundation

THE DAVID SUZUKI FOUNDATION works through science and education to protect the diversity of nature and our quality of life, now and for the future.

With a goal of achieving sustainability within a generation, the Foundation collaborates with scientists, business and industry, academia, government and non-governmental organizations. We seek the best research to provide innovative solutions that will help build a clean, competitive economy that does not threaten the natural services that support all life.

The Foundation is a federally registered independent charity that is supported with the help of more than fifty thousand individual donors across Canada and around the world.

We invite you to become a member. For more information on how you can support our work, please contact us:

The David Suzuki Foundation
219-2211 West 4th Avenue
Vancouver, BC Canada V6K 4S2
www.davidsuzuki.org
contact@davidsuzuki.org
Tel: 604-732-4228
Fax: 604-732-0752

Cheques can be made payable to The David Suzuki Foundation. All donations are tax-deductible.

Canadian charitable registration: (BN) 12775 6716 RR0001
U.S. charitable registration: #94-3204049